HANNAH BAKER'S FATAL FLAW

What You Need to Know
to Avoid Hannah's Fate

Fonda L. Hart, LMFT

Hannah Baker's Fatal Flaw:
 What You Need to Know to Avoid Hannah's Fate
© 2021 Fonda L. Hart

ISBN:

Cover and interior design: Marji Laine – Faith Driven Book Production
Poem, "Pretty Ugly," by Pakistani-American poet Abdullah Shoaib.

Printed in the United States of America.

Contents

Dear Reader,

Learning to adult today comes with more pressure, stress, and anxiety than ever before. Thanks to technology, not only do you live in a world where you have an overwhelming amount of freedom, you live in a world where everyone's "watching" the choices you make. And they don't let you forget them. As you go through your high school and even college years, so much is at stake when it comes to who you are and who you're going to be.

I wrote *Hannah Baker's Fatal Flaw* in hopes of helping people process the challenges they're facing in their own lives using the very serious issues Hannah Baker faces in *13 Reasons Why*. I want you to know life doesn't have to be dark or end without hope the way it did for Hannah. My wish is that this book will change the way you view yourself, show you that you have more control over your world than you think, and help you discover how to deal with your feelings, your friendships, your relationships, and the fallout from the decisions you make.

Fonda

who killed
hannah baker?

INTRODUCTION

*"You made it open season on
Hannah Baker."*

~Hannah Baker

Suicide. The word alone gives me an empty, kind of hollowed-out feeling. One I want to shake off but can't. *13 Reasons Why* isn't the easiest show to watch. As the season goes on, the episodes get more and more intense. And sadly, Hannah's life isn't completely out of the norm of what life in high school—and even middle school—looks like today. Girls, and guys too, struggle to keep standing, to keep moving forward under the weight of the pressures of social media, image, friends, relationships, parent and teacher expectations, their futures, and so much more.

Season 1 of *13 Reasons Why* starts with a student-made memorial on Hannah's locker as she narrates on the first tape. ". . . I'm about to tell you the story of my life." And ends with her conclusion that she had no choice but to end that life. But is that true? *Did* she really have no choice? Or did she have a choice? What happened in between, and who exactly is to blame?

I'm guessing several hundred students attend Liberty High.

The people in Hannah's story aren't all in one group of friends. They're people forced to go to the same place together every day—a group within a group—that in some way all play a part in Hannah's life and death. Throughout the tapes, we learn from Hannah that Justin and Jessica broke her heart. Alex, Tyler, Courtney, and Marcus helped destroy her reputation. Zach and Ryan broke her spirit. And Bryce broke her soul. To all them she says, "Some of you cared. None of you cared enough."

She was right about the beginning of that statement. Some of them did care. Others didn't. A few couldn't decide. And a couple were in the wrong place at the wrong time. Yet by the end, most everyone on the tapes comes to the same conclusion as Hannah—that they had something to do with her death.

Alex believes, "If any one of us had still been friends with her, she'd be alive today." Clay can't stop blaming himself. "I cost a girl her life because I was afraid to love her." Tony puts it on everyone involved, including Hannah. "She took her own life. That was her own choice. But you, me, everyone on these tapes, we all let her down. We didn't let her know that she had another choice. Maybe we could've saved her life, maybe not. It's impossible to know."

What are Alex, Clay, Tony, and the others really saying with the statement, "We all killed Hannah Baker"? What is Hannah saying by deciding she's done with life? That each person who hurt her or betrayed her was responsible for that moment she cut her wrists? That she couldn't have made any other choice?

The idea that someone holds that kind of power—the power of life or death—over someone else is terrifying. But is it true? Did each person who hurt Hannah cause her suicide? Was it all of them together? And does that mean that anyone who hurts us can push us into making the same tragic choice? Did Hannah have any power over her life and her death? Do we? If she had done anything differently with any of one of those 13 people, would she still be alive? What drives someone to take their own life? Is it one bad thing or two or three . . . or thirteen? Is it an impulsive moment or a path we step on and walk? There are so many questions. But all of them have answers.

The first episode starts with a short clip from a handful of the cast members. A sort of warning about watching the show and a place where you can get help if you, like Hannah, have your own reasons why. Alisha Boe, who plays Jessica Davis, leaves us with these words. "The minute you start talking about it, it gets easier."

Thats' what I want to do. I want to talk about it. Why? Because what happened to Hannah isn't just a story, and it comes with a powerful message. It just might not be the message you think.

The first season of *13 Reasons Why* is based on the book by Jay Asher. When he wrote it, he didn't imagine continuing the story. Because Netflix wanted several more seasons, they went on to "add events" to Hannah's tapes and to her timeline that were not part of the original story. That can get confusing when it comes to her original—and actual—reasons. For the purpose of this book, it makes sense to stay true to the original story and stick with Season 1. So that's what we're going to do.

Let's take a look at each of Hannah's reasons as she lays them out and figure out who's really responsible for her death. Because death is permanent. Forever. There is no reset button. No way to undo it. Hannah herself tells us there will be "No return engagements, no encore, and this time absolutely no requests." And I wonder if she'd given herself a little more time, gotten a little distance, or had some big-picture perspective if she wouldn't regret that one choice that took away all the others.

CHAPTER 1
JUSTIN FOLEY

"Justin, you were my kryptonite."
~ Hannah Baker

Justin is more or less an orphan. Sure, his mom's alive, but she's an addict with zero concern for her son and a violent boyfriend who has it out for him. The only thing we know about Justin's dad is that he's not in the picture.

Even kids with checked-out or workaholic parents have a place to crash and food in the fridge—or at least a way to pay for pizza. Not Justin. He truly has nothing, nowhere to go, and no one who cares. Yes, there's Bryce. But Bryce is only an option as long as Justin earns the friendship. On some level, we get that. For Justin, life is about survival.

Indecent Exposure

The night Justin and Hannah meet up at the park, he snaps a picture of her coming down the rocket slide. In that moment, it doesn't seem like he has bad intentions. They're playing and laughing like kids on the playground equipment. His actions don't feel like a set up. I see him as more of a lazy opportunist than a deliberate bad guy. But only Justin knows what's going on inside his own head.

If Hannah hadn't been wearing a skirt, her underwear wouldn't have been the focal point of that picture, and the story would've ended there. If Justin had deleted it, the story would've ended there. But that's not what happened.

The next day at school, Bryce asks Justin if he got to third base. Trying to be cool, he shows the picture to the guys and says, "A picture's worth a thousand words," using it as an opportunity to earn a little street cred. So not cool, Justin. Not cool at all. Especially because of what happens next. Bryce steals Justin's phone and shares that picture with most of the school. To be fair, that part wasn't Justin's fault. But violating Hannah's privacy and betraying her trust definitely was.

You might be thinking, *what? People take worse photos of themselves all the time and share them. Get over it already. That one little pic is no big deal.* But Hannah didn't take that photo. Hannah didn't post it. And if it hadn't been a big deal to her, she wouldn't have put Justin on her tapes as reason #1. The truth is that "one little pic" was:

- a jerk move
- a betrayal
- inappropriate
- disrespectful
- outside the realm of common decency
- sexual harassment

You may see that last point as a stretch, but it isn't. If you're blowing this off in your head, don't. Stick with me here for a bit because the picture that Justin took is what set off the landslide in Hannah's life. It's what gave her the "slut" reputation she didn't deserve. It's what allowed other guys to think they could use her. That picture is where Hannah believes her story started.

Legally, it was very much sexual harassment. Hannah could've and—I believe, should've—taken legal action. At the very least, she had the right to file a police report. But at the time, keeping quiet about it seemed the thing to do.

I realize that getting the police involved isn't "just that easy." It brings on its own issues. Even though it's the right thing to do, many people don't because of fear or because of what other people will think.

But did you know that if you file a police report without pressing charges, they don't usually take action? They keep the report in case something else happens or in case someone else presses charges. It's sort of like an insurance policy. If Hannah had filed a report, that paper trail would've held Justin *and* Bryce accountable, may have helped protect her reputation, and might've put a stop to future things that happened to her and other girls.

I wanted to point that out in case something happens to you. Hannah couldn't change what had already been done and neither can you, but you don't have to accept it as okay and keep quiet. You can do something about it. Here's how. If you want to file a report, call the non-emergency number for your local police department. The desk officer will give you information, answer questions, and help you set up a police visit. If you want to press charges, the process starts the same way.

If, like Hannah, you decide not to go that route, you can at least see a person's actions for what they are and stay away from them. Justin isn't the most trustworthy guy. Not as a friend. Definitely not as a boyfriend. How many chances should you give a guy like that? I'm thinking one is enough. If someone is worth having in your life, they won't take advantage of you, humiliate you, or use you to make themselves look better. Anyone who does those things probably doesn't belong anywhere near you. This might sound harsh, but it's true. And the sooner you cut off a relationship like that, the better off you'll be in the long run.

"Justin, You Were My Kryptonite"

Remember Superman? If you do, you probably also remember a thing or two about kryptonite, his famous weakness. If someone is your kryptonite, they make you lose your resolve. It's like saying, "I'm weak and at your mercy." Justin is Hannah's kryptonite. She wanted him to like her that badly.

The rocket slide at the park is her idea. It seems harmless on the surface. They're flirting on the phone. She doesn't want to let him be the one "who got away," so she jumps on the moment. That's kind of her trend with guys. And to be fair, she's not the only girl who struggles that way. It's like because she can't see her own worth and value, she's constantly looking for a guy to make her feel wanted and important. Your value isn't based on someone liking you or not liking you. This may seem obvious when I say it. But do you believe it? 'Cause that's a whole other thing.

Hannah tells Justin in this first tape, "I'm scared because I don't know how to fly. But you're there at the bottom of the slide to catch me when I fall." The guy is cute and popular and all, but Hannah doesn't really know what kind of person he is. Yet she's already molded him into her white knight.

By the way, just so you know, the only person who can really rescue you . . . is you.

Hannah sets up a whole scenario, fantasizing over their first kiss—her first kiss—and gives Justin power over her probably without even realizing it.

Common Sense 101 says not to give people power over you unless you know them, trust them, and have history with them. A person's track record gives you an idea of what to expect. What people have done in the past is generally a good indicator of what they'll do in the future. People don't just change. Not unless they have a really good reason. And I know you don't want to hear this, but that reason most likely won't be you. It takes a powerful set of circumstances to reconfigure how a person is wired. We actually see this later in Justin. But it's not because of who Hannah expected him to be.

Your "Yes" is Only as Good as Your "No"

Are you comfortable saying "no" when you want to? When's the last time you felt you should? Did you or didn't you?

Hannah needed to say "no" to herself. "No" to asking Justin to meet her in the park. "No" to her need to be liked by him. "No" to her insecurities. She could've waited to see him the next day at school. If he really liked her, he'd still like her in a few more hours. And if he didn't, she needed to know that sooner rather than later.

Even Superman knew to stay far, far away from kryptonite.

I don't know which is harder, saying no to yourself or saying no to someone else. There's an old book called *When I Say No, I Feel Guilty*. I think that about sums it up when it comes to setting limits with other people. Some of us don't say no because we feel guilty or anxious if we don't do what someone else wants. We worry about not being liked or making people mad or losing friendships or social status.

I won't lie. Your "no" might bring all those things on. But anyone who likes you for being you will accept you anyway. And whether you believe it or not, you want people to like you for being you. An emotionally healthy person can deal with not getting their way. What does that say about someone who can't? It says your "no" will always be a problem for them. Always is a long time.

What does it mean that your "yes" is only as good as your "no"? It means if you feel like you can't say no, how does a person know you mean it when you say yes? On the other hand, if you feel like you can say no but choose to say yes, your sincerity is real. "Yes," you do care about someone. "Yes," that relationship is important to you. People tend to trust someone who says "no" more than they trust someone who always says "yes."

Guys Like Girls Who Like Themselves (They Really Do)

When a girl tells a guy no, she's showing she can't be pushed around. Guys like that. No, for real, they do. No one wants someone who will do anything and everything they want. It may seem like they do at first, but when it comes down to it, that kind of person has nothing solid to bring to a relationship. A true relationship takes two people with feelings, opinions, and ideas.

If all a guy really wants is a quick hook-up, he's not looking for a relationship, and you aren't going to be the one to change his mind. If you're into commitment, that guy is not for you. It's worth knowing that guys who value themselves are into girls who value themselves. Those guys are out there, ladies. You just have to look for them. Up your standards. You're worth it.

Here's the cool thing about relationships and friendships— you can pick who you hang out with. Practice telling yourself "no" if you tend to get sucked into people who aren't good for you. Decide to find people who understand your "no" even if they don't like it. In the long run, you'll have a lot more peace with yourself, your relationships, and your friends.

I Want You to Want Me

Hannah didn't have much peace. She threw her self-esteem out there as an easy target. She admits on a later tape, "I always cared what other people thought of me as much as I acted like I didn't."

We all want to be wanted. Being wanted makes us feel like we deserve being liked and loved. Except . . . what gives other people the right to decide what we do or don't deserve?

When someone treats you badly, it's not okay. Ever. Some people will treat you that way as long as you let them—like you're their personal punching bag. But you don't have to stand there and take it. Walk away. Stick with people who care about you and like you for yourself.

You.

Are.

Precious.

If you saw the movie or read the book *The Help*, you'll remember the famous line, "You is kind. You is smart. You is important." Believe it. Be deliberate about it. Say it out loud. Put a Post-it on your mirror. Find your value and hang onto it as if it's your most important possession. In a way, it is. Your self-esteem isn't about anyone else. Don't give anyone else the power over how you feel about yourself.

Back to You, Hannah

What is Hannah's part in what went down with Justin? Please hear that I'm not throwing blame on the victim. That never helps anything. And I'm not picking on Hannah. But I'm thinking things could have been different for her. Maybe we can learn from her mistakes so things can be different for us.

I want to point out that along the way she had opportunities to make different decisions. That's where we can find our power—in our choices. Remember this if you're feeling helpless and out of control. Hannah shares something really smart when she says, "You can't change other people. But you can change yourself."

It's good to be cautious with people you don't know. Sometimes we accidentally set ourselves up to be taken advantage of. You can't always control what happens. But you can learn ways to protect yourself emotionally and physically. This is where boundaries come in. We all need them. Like a wall or a fence, they keep the good in and the bad out. When you're in situations that make you feel uncomfortable, it's more than okay to put yourself first and boundary up. Hannah didn't. And giving Justin so much power over her so quickly turned out to be not the best idea.

There's a difference between "responsibility" and "fault." If someone assaults you—or takes indecent photos or anything in between—that's not your fault. The person who did those things holds 100% of the blame. Let's be clear about that. That person is responsible for their own choices and actions.

Justin had the choice to be a decent person, and in that moment with Hannah, he failed. Hannah had the choice to make a better decision about who she trusted, and she didn't. It's not fair that Hannah could've made the same not-so-great choices with a different person and nothing would've happened. But life isn't fair. And neither are people. Not everyone plays by the "nice" rules. We sometimes forget that.

Don't blame yourself for what someone else did to hurt you. That will just put you in a downward spiral. But I think it's important to know that you can make decisions to protect yourself. You have more say in your life than you think. Hannah once asked, "It's my future. Don't I get a say in it?" Yes, Hannah, you absolutely do. And I wish you would've held onto that truth and exercised the option to the fullest.

What if Hannah . . .

- hadn't been in such a rush to be alone with Justin?
- had suggested someplace besides the park at night for a first "date" that wasn't even really a date?

- told Justin she wanted to introduce him to her parents? (Yes, I'm being for real)
- had gotten to know Justin at school before they were alone?
- had chosen to be friends first?
- hadn't let Justin kiss her so soon?
- had told her parents after the picture was posted?
- had taken legal action?

What if Hannah hadn't gotten stuck believing the people on the tapes were people she needed in her life? What if she'd known her worth, decided not to be friends with any of them, rescued herself, and found a different group instead? True friends.

Let's go back to Justin and Hannah. Justin gave Hannah her first kiss—something that's supposed to be wonderful and special. According to Hannah, it was. It's what came after that wasn't. It seems that moment at school, when Hannah realized Justin betrayed her and the gossip started, was the catalyst that pushed her toward the path to suicide. If I had a chance to talk to her before she took that first step, I'd tell her that life is so much more than one single situation. That you can choose to step onto a different path. That you don't have to let life happen to you. And that for some things, there are no second chances. Suicide is one of them.

CHAPTER 2
JESSICA DAVIS

"A hot-chocolate friendship. Maybe not good for all seasons."

~ Hannah Baker

Jessica is part of a military family that moves every two years. Even though she's used to being the new girl, it doesn't seem like that would be her first choice. Her dad seems strict but fair as does her mom, and she has two brothers. According to Hannah, Jessica is a nice girl. The kind of girl who becomes a cheerleader and ". . . the kind of girl boys like to like, not spread rumors about."

Both new to Liberty High sophomore year, Hannah and Jessica are called into Mrs. Antilly's office so she can set them up as friends because she doesn't want them to feel alone and overwhelmed. Even though Hannah says, "Do adults understand how friendships work?" she and Jessica instantly bond over the forced camaraderie. They hang out, shop, talk about boys, and spend a lot of time together at the local café—which is where they meet Alex, who is also new.

FML Forever

Misery loves company, right? Hannah, Alex, and Jessica declare "fml" every day after school at Monet's. It's what they have in common and what draws them together. When life gets hard, they have that mantra and each other.

Except for Jessica and Alex, "fml" describes their lives *in the moment*. That's important to point out. They want life to get better, and it does when they get together. Romance and "fml" don't usually go together. Dating generally makes you feel happier, more alive, more hopeful. Although their relationship is short-lived, it helps push them out of "fml." Not so much for Hannah.

"For A While, We Were the Kind of Friends You Wish You Had."

Hannah's friendship with Jessica and Alex clearly meant a lot to her. Several times throughout the tapes, we see her reaching out to get it back by suggesting a reunion at Monet's. But it never happens.

Alex is the first to leave their group. Jessica follows. According to Hannah, neither one says why. And she deeply feels the loss. Jessica tells Clay later that Hannah's a liar, and she left first. It's hard to know who to believe at that point because Jessica is living in major denial about what really happened to her the night of her party—and she needs to believe Hannah lied about that too. More on that when we get to Justin's second tape.

After Hannah finds out Jessica and Alex both abandoned the friendship so they could date, she's naturally hurt. It's obvious they're hiding their relationship when they show up at the theater on what was supposed to be her day off. Yes, they should've been honest. Most hurt feelings are the result of miscommunication and secrets. But at the same time, they didn't intentionally go behind her back and make a pledge to hurt her. They climbed out of their ruts, and she got left behind.

When Alex dumps Jessica—most likely because she won't sleep with him—she blames Hannah for the breakup. Because Alex leads Jessica to believe he hooked up with Hannah, Jessica runs with the gossip Justin started. "I know the rumors. How could you betray me like that . . . Enjoy it. 'Cause you will, won't you? That's what sluts do." That was brutal. Mean. Cruel. Totally uncalled for.

However you want to describe it, it upset Hannah and with good reason. Who wouldn't be hurt when someone they once trusted and shared themselves with calls them terrible names like "slut" and believes rumors over giving them the benefit of the doubt? The whole thing blows up from there with Hannah telling Jessica, "F*&% you," and Jessica retaliating with a slap.

Feelings Aren't Right or Wrong

Let's stop for a second and talk about feelings. Hannah had a right to be mad over the way Jessica treated her. Her feelings were valid. Our feelings are too. They're crucial to how we see and understand ourselves. Just so you know, there are no "good" or "bad" feelings. No "right" or "wrong" feelings. Feelings just are. Don't feel guilty or bad about having them. And don't listen when someone says, "you shouldn't feel that way."

I like to use my emotions as gauges that tell me about myself, kind of like the temperature and gas gauges in my car. I don't want the temperature to show "cool" or the gas to show "full" if the car's beginning to overheat or the tank is close to empty. I need the warning that something is wrong. That something has to be done if I want the car to keep running.

It's the same with feelings. It's important to know what we feel and to be honest about those feelings. Otherwise we won't know when something is going wrong. And if we don't know, we can't fix it. If we don't fix it, eventually we'll stop moving forward.

Unoffendable

Neither Hannah nor Jessica handled the Alex situation very well. Both of them could've made different choices about what they said and did. Jessica could've asked Hannah rather than accuse her. Hannah could've tried to explain. But I get it. Sometimes we get angry, and we go with the impulse to take that anger out on someone else. It's just too bad it had to go that way when there were other options. The situation could've been resolved with some better communication and a little grace for the other person.

Conflicts can be complicated. When we're in a "fight" with someone, we have this idea that if we don't get offended and angry it will look like the other person is right and we're wrong. Sometimes we believe that by not getting angry, we're saying what they did or said is okay. Not true. You can be right without going on the offensive. You can stand up for yourself or someone else without getting angry.

So why anger then? That's an easy one. It does something no other emotion does. It makes us feel powerful and in control. And that makes us feel safe. Imagine if anger was off the table. How would you feel instead? Hurt? Disappointed? Humiliated? Those emotions make us feel vulnerable. But like we talked about with the gauges on the car, dealing with our feelings works better if we see them and call them out for what they are.

It's sort of that old adage that admitting you have a problem is the first step to overcoming it. And you want to overcome it. Holding onto anger is bad for your brain and your body. Anger comes with boatloads of stress. Chronic stress increases a hormone called cortisol. Too much cortisol over a long time is toxic to your brain. It literally kills your brain cells.

I love this quote from the book *Unoffendable*. "If I don't need to be right, I don't have to reshape reality to fit 'The Story of My Rightness.' That makes life much easier, and makes us much more peaceful, and even fun to be around."

I'm not saying it's always bad to be offended. Sometimes we need to be. Bryce Walker is a jerk who disrespects every girl he meets. Look at how he grabbed Hannah's butt in the store. Hannah absolutely should've been—and was—offended. And what Jessica did to Hannah was horrible. In fact, Hannah was rightly offended by a number of people . . . which makes you wonder why she kept trying to be friends with them. Instead of staying in a relationship or a situation that constantly upset her, why didn't she move on and find nicer people? The harder question . . . why don't we?

Moving on or Staying Stuck

Changing yourself, your relationships, and the way you automatically react to things is hard. It's not something you decide to start one second and finish the next. It's a habit that needs to be reshaped. That takes work, time, patience, and commitment. But I promise it's so worth it.

I'm going to throw a few psych terms at you because that's my world. It's how I see things and relate to people. The book *Mindset* talks about a "growth mindset" versus a "fixed mindset." It's pretty self-explanatory. Someone with a growth mindset is open to growing. Someone with a fixed mindset isn't.

Say something negative—or even something that isn't negative but *feels* that way—to the first type of person and they think about it and learn from it. Even if it's hard. And it often is. Sometimes criticism is one percent right. Sometimes it's one hundred percent right. Ouch! That's the worst. The point is those with a growth mindset never stop trying to be better to those around them and to themselves—even if it's only that one percent. Why? Because they want to live "their best life," and they're running after it.

On the other hand, say the same thing to the second type of person and they can't or won't hear you. They're not running after their best life. They're not even walking. Instead, they stay firmly planted where they are and let you know, "This is all I am, all I've got, and I need to dig in to protect who I am." These people get defensive or lash out even if you're genuinely trying to help. And they stay stuck.

Every time I think about this idea, I picture a pond. Have you ever been around water that doesn't flow in or out and just sits there covered in algae? Unlike a spring or a stream where the water constantly moves and is clear and fresh, that pond stinks. You definitely don't want to touch or drink the water. When we refuse to move forward, we become stagnant like that pond. I see that a lot in Hannah.

When someone gives you constructive or not-so-constructive criticism, how do you handle it? Do you hear it or ignore it? Learn from it or get mad?

Feedback is different than rumors and gossip and words used like knives. You can't take those kinds of things back. There's a new more accurate twist on the old "sticks and stones" saying that goes, "Sticks and stones may break my bones, but words will break my heart." Isn't that the truth?

What if we set the bar higher? Upgraded how we treat people? Were intentional with our words? Maybe we'd start a new trend. Imagine if everybody changed how they talked to each other, ditched the gossip, and cut off the rumors? Wow. It'd be a whole new world—not just in high school but at home, at work, and where we hang out. And then those spaces might turn into places you actually like to be.

As Long as We Know Who to Blame

So . . . who *is* responsible for the destruction of Hannah and Jessica's friendship? I had a supervisor at work who used to say, "As long as we know who to blame, that's the important thing." She was joking, but her point was that it's better to own our mistakes and learn from them than to blame someone else. Blame does not make a bad situation better.

We each make our own choices, and we're responsible for those choices. Sometimes people make choices for us that we don't want. They walk away from relationships or get tired of a friendship and move on. No matter how much we want to, we can't control other people's choices. What we can control is how we respond. You're going to get tired of me saying that, but it's important.

In Jessica's case, she chose to move out of "fml" and into a different reality with Alex. They didn't necessarily need to leave Hannah behind to do that, but that's what they chose. Hannah chose to stay committed to "fml." Remember that fixed mindset? Any one of them could've started a conversation about the elephant in the room—Alex and Jessica as a couple—yet no one did.

Their choice took away a friendship Hannah wanted and thought she needed and left her only in control of what happened after—basically how she handled it. And she couldn't seem to let go. At least not in her heart. In light of that, both girls—and Alex—played a role in the destruction of their friendship.

This is a good place to touch on something else most people deal with in high school—wanting someone who doesn't want you or the other way around. It feels pretty awful when someone you like decides to like someone else, especially if that someone else is your friend. It's also super awkward when someone your friend likes decides to like you.

It's really too bad we can't change people's feelings. But we can't. You can't force love or attraction. You can't stop a person from liking someone or make them like you if they don't. Logically, that means there's no point in fighting over someone who doesn't have feelings for you. Except if you're the one left out, it sure doesn't feel that way.

When Girls Are Drama

I sometimes hear girls say they have issues with other girls because "girls are drama." Hannah had a reputation for being all about the drama. And sometimes she was. It's interesting that the people who complain the most about drama seem to be the same people creating the drama. Maybe if we all were a little slower to react, or chose not to overreact, a lot of it might go away.

Do you want to save yourself tons of emotional energy? I have a surefire way. Sidestep drama. Refuse to get upset. Walk away when you want to fight back. Yes, easier said than done, but want to hear something that makes sense? The author of the book *Triggers* says that getting mad at people for being who they are is like being mad at a chair because it's a chair.

Huh . . .

When you put it that way . . .

Sidestepping drama might mean we need to change up our relationship with a particular "chair." A person is who they are whether we want to accept it or not. Eventually, we're going to have to be okay with that. We may even have to accept that we don't like them anymore, and it's best to walk away. Letting go can be rough. Especially if we really wanted that person in our lives.

I've learned something over the years. Thinking about breaking up with someone, whether it's a romantic relationship or a friendship, can hurt more than actually doing it. In a weird way, there's relief after the whole thing is said and done. I think because it's freeing to be able to put the relationship behind you, be sad and grieve the loss, and start moving forward.

Hannah couldn't seem to do that with Jessica. She was always trying to rekindle the friendship even if it came back to hurt her. Clay chose to stick out his friendship with Hannah. But in order to do that, he had to accept that she didn't have great boundaries when it came to guys. And that was hard for him to watch. Jessica eventually chose to let go of Justin. She acknowledged that even though he loved her, he devastatingly failed to protect her when she most needed it, and she didn't want that kind of person in her life.

You Got to Know When to Hold 'Em and When to Fold 'Em

Forgiveness. A loaded word. Here's what I want you to know. If you choose to forgive, it's not the same as saying the way someone treated you is okay or that you are accepting the blame for what went wrong. But whether you stay in a relationship or not, it is better for you to let go of resentment and anger.

Better for you. Did you get that part?

Why? Because as unfair as it sounds, you're the one who pays the price for holding a grudge—not the person you're angry with—and it's not worth the energy it will cost you. Unforgiveness is a ticking time bomb that leads to bitterness. Bitterness eats at you from the inside out. It's for your own mental health that you need to "Shake it off." Just ask Taylor Swift.

Back to You, Hannah

We already talked about where Hannah had control in this situation—in how she handled it. In how much she let Jessica's choices hurt her. She couldn't stop Jessica and Alex from deserting the friendship. That's true. But she could've protected her heart better after they left and learned to protect it better in the future. Like we said before, the choices other people make that affect you aren't fair. But fair can be a unicorn sometimes, can't it? Sometimes we just have to deal with the hurtful choices people make and decide what we're going to do with them.

Hannah let others define her. She kept going back to the people who hurt her. She made the same mistakes over and over—after she said she was going to change. She didn't seem to learn from bad experiences, which both held her back in life and pushed her forward on that path to suicide. The scary thing is, she never realized she was even walking that path until the end.

FONDA L. HART

CHAPTER 3
ALEX STANDALL

"Little did I know you would f my l forever."

~ Hannah Baker

For having a cop for a father, Alex isn't quite what you'd expect. He's a musician. He's a little different. Has his own style. And on the outside seems like a nonconformist. On the inside, he cares more about what the other guys think about him than he wants to. And that gets him into trouble.

Alex really makes a mess of things with both Hannah and Jessica. When Bryce and the others believe Alex and Jessica are having sex, he not only goes with it, he thinks because it's already been assumed a "thing," they should be. But Jessica's not on board. And that's where that stupid list comes in.

The List

After Jessica rejects Alex, he gets back at her by adding her name to Bryce's list as "worst butt." Not only that, he adds Hannah as "best butt." That's what leads Jessica—and everyone else—to believe he and Hannah hooked up.

Hannah says of the list, "It was an assault on my personhood." And she's not wrong. There's a weird—and sad—irony in a "Who's Hot and Who's Not" list. Being labeled "hot" is a creepy compliment that secretly might make me feel good. Being labeled "not hot" is an outright insult that would definitely make me feel bad even if I tried to blow it off. And what if I'm not on the list at all? Does that make me a nobody? I think I'd be offended that the list exists and hurt that I didn't count enough to be on it.

Sit Still, Look Pretty

Angie Romero, voted "best lips," is able to laugh off the list. Hannah isn't. But then again, people staring at your butt feels way more personal than people staring at your lips. Bryce's list was meant to objectify or humiliate the girls on it—depending on which column he put them in.

What exactly is objectification? And as girls—and guys—do we care about it? In "Sit Still, Look Pretty," Daya talks about not putting on makeup or playing dumb to get a boy who'll treat her like a toy. She tells us she could dress up to get love but that she's never gonna be that girl living in a Barbie world. Instead, she wants to be the girl who rules the world.

Objectification degrades you to the status of an object. A decoration. A dumb blonde. Maybe eventually a trophy wife. And yes, you should care about it. It's a little too easy to take on the way others treat us as truth. And that can lead to some dangerous thoughts like, *If others don't respect me as a person, why should I respect myself?* This is a loose definition of self-objectification which comes with some pretty awful consequences. Like eating disorders and self-harm and depression. On the other hand, if you don't respect yourself, why would others respect you? So, I'm with Daya. I have no intention of just sitting still and looking pretty.

Toxic Masculinity

Since we're dealing with the topic of objectification, let's talk about "toxic masculinity." They're connected. A lot of guys "suffering from" toxic masculinity are the same guys who objectify girls. We're focusing on guys here, however girls can be toxic too—just usually in different ways. Both can cause equal destruction.

I'm guessing because you live in the middle of the #metoo age, you might already have an idea what toxic masculinity is. We used to call guys like this macho. The Village People had a song about it in 1978. The lyrics to "Macho Man," are funny. But they're also not.

The New York Times put out an article in 2019 that equates toxic masculinity to someone who cuts off their emotions, hides their feelings, and even uses violence to show their power. Think tough guy. No, not the kind in YA romance where the girl breaks down the bad boy's walls and they fall in love and he becomes a different person and . . . ya da, ya da, ya da . . . happily ever after.

No, these are the guys who beat up other guys, catcall girls, bully everyone, start fights, and may even become the school shooter. As I'm writing this chapter, there have been several mass-shooting attempts in the last few months. All the shooters have been male.

There's nothing wrong with being a "manly" guy in and of itself. There's a lot about it that's pretty awesome. In several of those attempted shooting incidents, men who legally "carried concealed" acted courageously. By taking down the shooters, they saved dozens—and, in one case, hundreds—of lives. Someone called this "non-toxic masculinity." I call it masculinity at its best.

True masculinity is about courage and self-sacrifice. Pay a tiny amount of attention if you're taking History. The past has proven this. There are men of great character who make a difference in the world. And there are women of great character who do the same.

Most Guys Are Decent

Bryce created "The List." Are we surprised? I'm shaking my head no. Alex took the bait and added to it. So did a few other guys. Yep, that sounds about right. But did every guy who saw the list add to it? Again, I'm shaking my head. Some guys glanced at it and passed it on. There *are* decent guys out there who would've ignored the list. Guys who don't objectify girls. Yes, they might've read it. But they didn't fuel it. Clay was one of those.

Eventually even Alex wants to take back his contribution, genuinely regretting the part he played in costing Hannah her friendship with Jessica. Unlike most of the others on the tapes, he isn't just out for himself and admits, "Everything Hannah said on the tapes is true." He tells Clay he was "that guy" who tried to have sex with Jessica. "I ruined the one good thing I had." I liked Alex for seeing his mistakes and wanting to tell the truth. And it was hard to watch him come to the same decision as Hannah and attempt suicide because he couldn't take the secrets and lies. I'm just glad he survived his attempt.

Social Learning Theory

As the list is passed around, Mrs. Bradley's class is discussing Social Learning Theory. But that discussion doesn't accurately represent what the theory is all about. If you go by that clip, you come away thinking that one person has the power to influence a whole group of people, for better or for worse. Basically, we make crappy choices just because we see crappy choices being made.

You can see how Hannah gets distracted by that "pied piper" view and convinces herself that because of the list she's doomed to be seen by everyone as nothing but a butt. In reality, though, that's a little too "all or nothing" and not quite what Social Learning Theory is all about.

What it is about is the importance of watching someone else learn new things. It's that "watching" of what someone's doing, how they're doing it, and their feelings about it that helps us learn. I'm sure you've heard the term "reinventing the wheel." Well, imagine if we had to learn everything by doing it without ever having seen it done before. Life would be much more difficult and frustrating.

Going with this idea of Social Learning Theory, at any time, any one person could've put a stop to Bryce's list. Someone could've torn it up or chosen not to pass it on or even showed it to an adult. Hey, it could happen. Mrs. Bradley would've been a good person to give it to.

If the other students had seen someone else try to shut down that list, several of them would likely have let it go themselves. Some people are able to stand up for themselves and others. Some are afraid of rocking the social boat and choose to follow the crowd instead. But I've discovered that when even just one person does the right thing, more likely than not, others will be relieved and will follow their lead.

When the Whole Is Greater Than the Sum of the Parts

Back to the list and objectification. Does $2 + 2$ ever add up to more than 4? It does when we're talking about what makes us "us." People are more than their parts.

I'm pretty sure most us want to be seen as attractive and appealing—especially to someone we like or love. That's totally normal. But we also want to be seen for who we are not just how we look. We're so much more than a body.

Want to hear something interesting about supermodels? When asked what they like about their bodies, they often name obscure things rather than the obvious traits the public notices. One supermodel listed her calves as her favorite body part. Her calves! Really? Um . . . okay.

Some of these models laugh at their airbrushed images in ads—because they know they don't look like that in real life. Only about 5% of the population even has the anatomy to look remotely like a supermodel. But we don't think about that as we're scrolling through their posts. We just think about how perfect they look and how not perfect we feel.

True Beauty

What if we were to value people for *who they are* instead of *what they look like*?

Was Jessica pretty? Yes.

Was Hannah pretty? Yes.

Were both their butts attractive? I'm sure they were.

We could find surface beauty in each person the guys put on the "hot" list. But true beauty is personal and unique and, as the saying goes, "in the eye of the beholder." The list robs each of the people on it from loving all of who they are.

The beauty industry is a multibillion machine that dictates what beauty is and isn't—for one purpose—so we'll buy their products in an attempt to become something we aren't and don't need to be.

We don't just buy their products. We buy the lie that we're not okay if we have or don't have certain attributes. We spend money we don't have for things we don't need. Why? To make us more attractive. Or at least to make us *feel* more attractive. The newness of the thing we buy gives us a high . . . until it wears off, and we need the next new thing. Classic retail therapy. And it's not just girls who feel this way. Guys stress over their bodies and their looks too. They can feel just as inadequate.

No person can define you as beautiful or ugly. But some things are universally attractive. No, not what you think. I'm talking about confidence and being real. People who are comfortable in their own skin are people we want to be around. Why? Because those are the kind of people who seem to forget their imperfections and "live" in the moment, happy with where and who they are.

When you meet someone, what do you notice first? What's important to you? Personality? Sense of humor? How they treat people? Or do you only see a body? It's entirely normal to notice looks, but if that's as far as you go, you may be in for a string of unsuccessful relationships before you find anything real. True beauty is more than skin deep.

Guys, have you ever met a girl who was more than a few numbers off from a ten, but something about her drew you in? Girls, have you ever traded a serious set of abs for trustworthy character and an easy-going personality? Twentieth Century American president Theodore Roosevelt said, "Comparison is the thief of joy." Be okay with who you are. Be real, and you'll attract real people.

Little Did I Know . . .

Hannah hasn't known Alex very long when he adds her butt to the list. Yet she says, "Little did I know you would fml forever. Little did I know you would be my hurricane." Let's take those two statements one at a time.

All I can say about the first is, *wow—forever?* Fml? We've all been there. Fml forever? That's when you're straight up stuck. Hannah wanted life to be better. I truly believe that. Only how can you make things better if you're committed to fml forever? Those two ideas cancel each other out.

And the second? What Hannah's really saying is that Alex set off a chain of events that led to her complete destruction. Seriously, Hannah? There's no way Alex had that kind of power over your life. You weren't childhood friends. You weren't dating. You didn't have that kind of history.

On Alex's tape, Hannah talks about the Butterfly Effect as if it were a scientific fact that determined her destiny, using it to validate and romanticize her suicide. Let me tell you, there is nothing romantic about suicide. Tony came face-to-face with that when he watched the paramedics. "And they just grabbed the body bag and threw her in the ambulance."

Think about that a second. Hannah went to all that work making the tapes, tying up loose ends, returning her uniform, making her bed, and even changing into old clothes to avoid ruining her good clothes. Those days and hours leading up to her death, she was painstakingly meticulous and careful—just so her body could be carelessly tossed into the back of a truck. I don't think she saw that coming.

The Real Butterfly Effect

If a butterfly flaps its wings in Brazil, will it set off a tornado in Texas? Meteorology professor Edward Lorenz first asked that question at a science convention in 1963, and the concepts behind it are still used today to generate daily weather forecasts. It's called Chaos Theory. But it doesn't mean what Hannah thought. There may be a hurricane, but it's not directly related to the butterfly. And besides, that would be impossible to trace. The Butterfly Effect is simply a metaphor used to describe a mathematical concept.

Let's pull this concept into real life. If you're the butterfly, does flapping your wings affect the person next to you and the person next to them and so on? Only to a certain degree. Hannah felt the tornado of other people. At some time or another, we all have. The question isn't whether our decisions affect others. The answer will always be, *of course they do*. The question is, how will we respond to those decisions? Or even, how much will we let them affect us?

Do I have to continue what someone "flaps" to me? Nope. Unlike the butterfly in Brazil, that has no control over external forces such as the jet stream, a nuclear explosion, or a tsunami, we have the power to decide how we handle what's going on around us.

This poem by Benjamin Franklin reminds me of the Butterfly Effect.

> For the want of a nail the shoe was lost,
> For the want of a shoe the horse was lost,
> For the want of a horse the rider was lost,
> For the want of a rider the battle was lost,
> For the want of a battle the kingdom was lost,
> And all for the want of a horseshoe-nail.

For the lack of a nail, you can't shoe the horse. But duh, nothing's stopping you from getting a different horse. The power to change the outcome belongs to us. Not the nail. Not the horse. Us. This is the real Butterfly Effect.

What impact do you want to have on the world? On the people around you? On your friends and family? You're far more powerful than a butterfly. You can choose whether to be a positive or negative impact, whether to build relationships or isolate, and how you spend your time. What legacy will you leave? If you're a Lord of the Rings fan, you'll recognize this saying by Gandalf. "Even the smallest person can change the course of the future." It's true. I've seen it.

Every Step Leads Somewhere

"The journey of 1000 miles begins with a single step." Have you ever heard that ancient Chinese proverb? In other words, you won't get anywhere or accomplish anything without taking the first step. At the same time, every step—every choice you make—moves you in one direction or another, toward life and happiness or death and destruction.

Imagine sailing a boat from San Francisco to Hawaii. That's a 2,400-mile journey. You'll need your compass. If you simply follow the winds and the current, you'll get lost at sea. To arrive in Hawaii instead of New Zealand, you'll need to constantly reevaluate and readjust your course. It's the same with life. If you want to get somewhere, you have to set goals and keep putting one foot in front of another while you're reevaluating and readjusting your course.

Back to You, Hannah

Hannah was so focused on one group of people—one small segment of the school—that she couldn't see the big picture. What if she had been able to see more than just what was happening in the moment? What if she would've zoomed out and gotten a wider perspective? What if the next time things got hard, you zoomed out?

Alex really let Hannah down. But were his immature and insensitive actions worth another step on her path to suicide?

No.

Absolutely no.

I wish she would've realized that life is so much more than the selfish, stupid actions of a few friends. Here's one other thing I've been noticing about Hannah. She didn't seem to realize she wasn't the only one struggling. Yes, she wanted to relate to other people and bond over things they were both experiencing. But she so often made it all about her. Like she expected a one-sided loyalty that didn't leave room for what anyone else wanted or needed.

Everyone has issues. They can't spend all their time dwelling on the gossip and rumors spreading about someone else. But in Hannah's mental map, she feels as though everyone is constantly watching and judging her, as if the world is revolving around her. That's a loose definition of something called "self-referentiality" where, in her mind, everything refers back to Hannah.

Even if it seemed like it, the entire school wasn't focused on that list. Most people wouldn't have been interested even if they saw it, and not every guy added to it. Life might've changed for Hannah if she'd been able to blow off the list for what it was—a waste of her time and energy.

Hannah's suicide was not as inevitable as she made it sound. She did have options. She just couldn't see them. No choice is inevitable. "Choice" and "inevitable" are contradictions. If you can choose suicide, you can choose life.

Each drastic step she took was within her control. In fact, she was the only one who could control her choices. Hannah chose death over life. Drama over reason. Devastation to those who loved her over forgiveness to those who didn't. And that breaks my heart.

MIRROR, MIRROR

When you look into the mirror, what do you see? It's a trick question—of course, you see you. But is your reflection all of who you really are? And what about what's below the surface? Can you even see beyond what runs skin deep?

Mirrors, as we know them, have only existed since the early 1800s. Before that, dating back to ancient times, they were made of polished metal or stone, and only the very wealthy could afford to own one. That means you could go through your entire life without ever seeing yourself.

Imagine only knowing what you look like based on how other people describe you. Depending on who those other people are, you might get a different description every time. Someone's appearance is subjective and based on the observer's experience and bias. A person who's critical of double chins might see the hint of one in you regardless of your weight and size. And if other people are defining you, not only are you at their mercy, but how do you know if what they say is true?

If you've ever gone into a fun house at a fair, you've probably looked into a distorted mirror that shows your neck longer than your legs. At least we know that image isn't real, and we can laugh it off as an illusion. But feedback from people is harder to throw away. Sometimes we take in distorted mirroring from others who don't really see us as we are or who don't have our best interests at heart.

Don't Be Humiliated by Something That Isn't True

Nobody enjoys hearing negative things about themselves. Especially things that aren't true. People sometimes talk just to talk. And they're mean just to be mean. There's a new anti-bullying strategy being taught in some schools. Instead of being intimidated by or taking on what's been said, kids are taught to self-mirror more accurately. This helps them from dwelling on the lies that bullies tell.

"Self-mirroring" is an important life skill that can save you a lot of pain. Not a pep talk exactly, this idea is more like calling upon what you know is true about yourself and then using it as emotional protection. It's throwing away negative thinking and embracing the power of positive thinking. But it works best if you have the courage to be honest with yourself.

Here's how it works. If someone told you, "You're stupid," instead of immediately owning your stupidity and dragging up every other time you feel like you've been stupid, you think it through. *I'm getting good grades. I got an A on my math test and a B+ on that history project. My parents are proud of me. My friends ask me for help with their homework. So . . . stupid huh?*

Nope. That doesn't fit. And even better, I'm not stupid, I'm actually kind of smart."

Do you see how it works? You take the truth of who you are and compare it with what someone else has said. Let's try another one. If someone told you, "You're weird," you refrain from taking that on and take a breath. *Other kids like me. I get along with my family and my friends. I'm not doing anything weird. I act normal. Weird, no. That's not true. I'm okay, and I'm likable.* Or you might even realize, *yeah, I'm a little eccentric but in a good way. I'm not buying that I'm weird. I prefer unique. And unique is a good thing. I don't blindly follow the crowd.*

Go ahead. Give it a try. Condition yourself not to be susceptible to the opinion of others. Work on being strong in who you are. Don't let people tear you down. By self-mirroring, you really have everything to lose—in the very best way. You lose the heaviness of someone's hurtful lies when you ditch what they say. In fact, if something said to you or about you isn't true, don't waste time and energy defending yourself. In other words, if the big, clunky, ugly shoe doesn't fit, don't even try to wiggle it on.

But What if the Shoe Does Fit?

What happens if what someone says is true or partially true? You have options. Work through it. Look at their feedback as objectively as you can. Ask yourself what might be true and what might not be true. Only accept what you know to be accurate and throw the rest away. Then you can deal with what you need to deal with and change what needs to be changed. Remember, constructive criticism can help you grow and improve.

On the Flip Side

Sometimes we're guilty of distorting someone else's mirror. There are times when we tend to believe the worst about someone and forget about giving them the benefit of the doubt. What's worse is that while we're doing that, we still want them to believe the best about us. But it doesn't work that way. You can't assume the worst about people and expect them to believe the best about you.

Just like you should surround yourself with people who will mirror accurately to you, you need to do the same for them. Wouldn't it be great if we all saw each other's beauty and at the same time weren't aren't afraid to call each other out on the important things in a caring way?

Find people who truly like you and bring out the best in you—not because they make you believe you're better than you are but because they mirror you honestly. A good friend will say not just what you want to hear, but what you *need* to hear. Even painful words of truth are better than inauthentic flattery, because if what others say about you isn't true, it's meaningless. When you're seen for who you really are, you're free to be yourself. Imagine if we all could live that way.

Social Media Mirroring

A lot of people who've grown up with social media let it define who they are. It's easy to fall into the trap of defining yourself by the number of "likes" or "comments" given by virtual friends—people who may not even know you for who you really are.

Some people post countless selfies, as if they need the constant mirroring of others telling them "You're okay, you're beautiful, you're amazing." It's a rush, yes. Those kinds of things cause a dopamine surge in our brains, but one that doesn't last. And as soon as it wears off, we need our next "fix" of social media mirroring. I'm always impressed when I meet someone who has decided not to use social media.

Here's an interesting statistic: the increase in depression and self-harm among teen girls directly correlates with when iPhones hit the market. I'm not blaming Apple, but I am pointing out that constant exposure to social media makes us more insecure and more susceptible to what others think of us. In some ways, we're not better off for having smartphones.

The Mirror Within

It's important to have an internal "mirror," not just when it comes to dealing with bullies, but when it comes to life. Being able to step outside yourself and "observe" who you really are has a huge impact on how you feel about yourself and your world.

Can you say things like this to yourself? If not, make a point to try. "Yeah, I'm a little shy, but I'm also kind of cool. I should go to drama tryouts and not be afraid of people." "Wow, look at how loud I'm talking to that person. I should tone it down." "I really feel like punching this person right now, but I just need to step back."

Remember the wicked queen in Snow White? She wanted the mirror to follow a script and tell her she was "the fairest of them all" with no regard for whether it was true or not. You can live in a fantasy world if you want, but that doesn't change the truth.

When the mirror finally called it and said, "There is one who is more beautiful than you…" the queen couldn't handle it. And since she had zero self-mirroring skills, she couldn't tell herself, "Hey Majesty, you're getting a little out of control here. The problem isn't Snow White's beauty. It's your jealousy." Had the queen been able to see that, she might not have resorted to attempted murder and she might still be alive today.

I know that's silly. She's just a fairytale character. But hopefully, you get the idea. Did you know that being willing to look deeply into yourself also helps you keep a clear conscience? We can feel guilty over so many things. Even things we haven't done wrong. But if you take a minute now and then to check yourself, you'll be able to own what you should and release what you shouldn't.

Be Kind to Yourself

My friend Kent Ostby wrote, "One of the single biggest changes you can make in your life is to talk to your self the same way you would talk to the person you love the most. Talk to yourself the way you would encourage your niece, nephew, son, daughter, friend. What would you say? You would acknowledge a mistake and then ask how they could do it differently next time or teach them how to do it differently next time. Give yourself that gift. You will make mistakes so when you do, coach yourself up for the next adventure or to-do."

Change Your Perspective, Change Your Life

Here's a clever poem by Pakistani-American poet Abdullah Shoaib. Abdullah is studying to be a high school math teacher and is a budding freelance writer. The poem is titled "Pretty Ugly." Whether it's one or the other depends on your perspective.

Pretty Ugly

I'm very ugly
So don't try to convince me that
I am a very beautiful person
Because at the end of the day
I hate myself in every way
And I'm not going to lie to myself by saying
There is beauty inside of me that matters
So rest assured I will remind myself
That I am a worthless, terrible person
And nothing you say will make me believe
I still deserve love
Because no matter what
I am not good enough to be loved
And I am in no position to believe that
Beauty does exist within me
Because whenever I look in the mirror I always think
Am I as ugly as people say?

But don't stop here. This next part is the most IMPORTANT. Read it again from the BOTTOM UP. Yep. Start with the last line and read straight to the top. Better yet, read it out loud standing in front of the mirror.

Quite a contrast in perspective, isn't? How did you feel reading it the first time? How did you feel reading it "backward"? Did anything shift inside you? Did it change the way you think of yourself? Sometimes the way you look at things can change everything.

FONDA L. HART

HANNAH BAKER'S FATAL FLAW

CHAPTER 4
TYLER DOWN

"Nowhere was safe. You took all that away."
~ Hannah Baker

Thoughts on Tyler? Did you find him creepy? Did you feel sorry for him? I think we can all agree that he's definitely "off." An interesting contradiction, Tyler is both the awkward nerd who doesn't fit in and the creepy watcher who disregards everyone's privacy. His crush on Hannah upgrades him to the role of stalker.

He doesn't really seem to want to hurt anyone . . . except when he does. He comes off as though he thinks he's smarter than everyone else . . . except he's missing some major insight. And he's predictably unpredictable. That can be scary for those around him. If you watch more than the first season of *13 Reasons Why*, you'll see exactly what I mean.

Protect Yourself

Even though Tyler's violent streak doesn't come out until Season 2, let's take a time-out to talk about guys like Tyler. With unpredictable people, the best idea is to keep your distance. You

— 57 —

don't really want anything to do with them.

But at the same time, don't pretend the Tylers of the world don't exist. If you notice something odd or strange that makes you anxious or uncomfortable, please, please, please say something to someone who can step in before the situation gets too bad—parents, teachers, counselors, principles, police, or any adult you trust.

It's a bad idea to ignore your "gut." Don't be afraid of being wrong. Don't keep quiet. Go with that saying, "If you see something, say something." It's always better and smarter to say something and find out it's nothing than to wish you'd spoken up later. If you're worried you'll be outed, ask to remain anonymous. If you tell a trustworthy person, they'll keep where they got their information a secret. And remember, you can't always count on others to watch out for you. But you can watch out for yourself and, by doing so, keep other people safe as well.

The Chicken or the Egg

We may not know all the ins and outs of Tyler, but we do know what people thought of him. Courtney sums it up perfectly when Tyler threatens to tell everyone about the tapes. "You can do whatever you want. People will just laugh at you like they always do."

You know the saying, "Which came first, the chicken or the egg?" In Tyler's case, it's more "Who's reacting to who?" Does he get bullied because he acts weird and provokes people? Or does he act weird and provoke people because he gets bullied?

After Tyler gets pantsed, he says, "I don't understand why I'm the one always getting screwed with." Mr. Porter asks Tyler what he can do to protect himself and if there's anything he's doing to provoke other kids. Unable to see his part in anything that happens to him, he responds, "That's convenient. Blame the victim." Remember when we talked about the difference between "responsibility" and "fault"? Tyler just does not get that.

He sees himself as the victim or the hero. But never the perpetrator. People like Tyler often don't recognize the lines they're crossing. When Clay calls him out for taking pictures of Hannah, telling him he's a criminal and a creep, Tyler responds with, "I'm the student life photographer. I stalk everybody. It's my job." Um . . . sure, Tyler. Whatever you say. You know those boundaries we talked about earlier? Tyler doesn't get them. At all. And that's a huge problem. Not knowing where to draw the line leaves other people weirded out and nervous.

Peeping Tom . . . Er . . . Tyler

Tyler most likely has a disorder called voyeurism. A voyeur thinks about or wants to spy on others while they undress or have sex. Super creepy, right? And very gross. Voyeurs are so consumed with this sexual need that it doesn't occur to them that they're violating or hurting the people they're watching. That cluelessness makes Tyler more dangerous because he doesn't understand why people are upset. And that makes *him* upset. His excuse for stalking Hannah? "I loved her." Stalking is so not love.

In fact, let's take this a bit further. If someone gets into your phone or social media or intercepts your messages or emails, this is cyberstalking. It's illegal. And it's a definite sign you need to get away from them. Emotionally health people don't need to intrude like that.

Criminal Invasion of Privacy

When Clay confronts Tyler, he mentions criminal invasion of a minor's privacy, pointing out, ". . . the first offense is only six months in jail. But for repeat offenders, that's a year." He's right. Except the law actually calls it "criminal invasion of privacy." Period. The law isn't specific to minors. And in some states, the first offense comes with a $1,000 fine.

And just so we're clear, Tyler's actions fall under that law. Spying on Courtney and Hannah outside her window was illegal. Don't minimize that just because it seems like he could've done much worse. What he did was absolutely not okay. Hannah could've prosecuted. Courtney could've as well.

When Justin took the photo of Hannah on the slide and Bryce posted it, that was a criminal invasion of her privacy. Same when Clay took the nude of Tyler and sent it to everyone. Even if you see Clay as the good guy in this, he still broke the law. You might be thinking Tyler deserved the payback, but revenge carries a price. If Tyler had gotten the police involved, it could've gone very badly for Clay.

Real Safety Versus *Felt* safety

This time for Hannah, it wasn't about a picture going viral. "But then, the pictures you took that night aren't the reason you're on this tape, are they?" It was about how Tyler made her feel.

"Even after you stopped coming around, I never stopped feeling afraid . . . even in my own bedroom."

There is a difference between "real" safety and "felt" safety. Real safety is being out of danger. Felt safety is feeling like you are safe. Obviously, *real* safety is crucial. In this situation, real safety involves Tyler no longer stalking Hannah. But here's something important to understand. Invasion of privacy robs us of *felt* safety. She needed to feel safe to move on. But she never knew whether Tyler would return—because she never turned him in.

It's so important to tell someone if you're being stalked. By telling your parents and friends and calling the police, you bring "power" into the process and show the violator that:

- you're not helpless
- you're not isolated
- you're not going to be pushed around
- they will be held accountable

Since "doing the right thing" doesn't seem to be high on a stalker's priority list, keeping it to yourself and asking them to back off probably isn't going to work. But the fear of being caught and prosecuted might. Or it might not. But you aren't helpless, and you don't have to be alone. Protect yourself by getting other people involved.

Several years ago, I worked with a support group for young kids who had lots of anxiety. Some had school-related fears, some had issues at home, some were getting bullied, and some worried about *everything*. One of the skills we taught them was that there are three types of fears—real, exaggerated, and imaginary.

Imaginary fears are being afraid there are monsters under your bed. Fears that are impossible. Monsters don't exist. I can guarantee you there are no literal monsters under your bed.

Exaggerated fears are being afraid you'll be in a plane crash or get kidnapped. It could happen, but it's highly unlikely.

Real fears are, well, real. They could happen. If you live in a tornado zone and there's a tornado warning, your home could be flattened by a storm. If you're camping, you could get bitten by a poisonous spider.

We taught the kids with imaginary and exaggerated fears how to deal with calming exercises and positive thinking. We gave them tools to use so they could understand that they already had real safety—they just needed to *feel* it.

But for the kids with real fears, it wasn't about *feeling* safe. It was about *being* safe. We helped these kids come up with a plan to deal with a situation in the event it actually happened. In many cases, that meant asking for help.

I think these tools work for every age. Once you figure out which category your fear fits into, you can take it on and bring it down to size.

Tyler *was* a real Peeping Tom. Had Hannah involved her friends, her parents, or the police, as soon as the lack of *felt safety* kicked in, she could've gotten help to realize she was safe.

Counseling helps too. There's a cool kind of therapy out there called EMDR that desensitizes fears. I've found it to be a powerful tool for taking the "charge" out of traumatic events. We'll talk more about it later.

Back to You, Hannah

Yes, Tyler is creepy and intrusive and voyeuristic. Sane people do not hide in bushes and spy on people. But on the flip side, most of us close our blinds at night—especially if our window faces the street like Hannah's did and definitely when we're getting undressed! As soon as she realized someone was outside, she could have:

- closed the blinds
- locked the windows and doors
- set the alarm
- told her parents and/or her friends
- called the police

Hannah had a right to feel safe again. Everyone should feel safe in their own home. And there are things she could've done to make that happen. But she didn't. And that's tragic. Considering how caring Hannah's parents were, I'm certain they would've jumped in to help her. If she'd gotten the police involved, Tyler might've done prison time and been fined. And that would've stopped a whole bunch of other bad stuff from going down. Based on that *first* incident alone, he would've had to register as a sex offender. That's a powerful deterrent to stalking right there.

Hannah had enough power over Tyler's life to hold him accountable. Yet she didn't. What's worse is that she eventually punished herself for what he—and all the other people on the tapes—did to her. By ending her life, she gave herself the death penalty for crimes she didn't commit.

FONDA L. HART

CHAPTER 5
COURTNEY CRIMSEN

"You are just so . . . nice. Right? Wrong."
~ **Hannah Baker**

The first time Hannah and Courtney get together things turn sexual. When Courtney comes over to help set a trap for Hannah's stalker, they plan to hang out in her bedroom and leave the blinds open to catch him in the act. Then they start drinking . . . which leads to a game of Truth or Dare . . . which leads to other things.

Hannah dares Courtney to take another drink. Yelling, "Boring," she dares Hannah to take off her bra under her shirt. Not to be outdone, she dares Courtney to take off her shirt. Courtney comes right back with, "I dare you to kiss me." When Hannah laughs it off, Courtney pushes the idea, and they kiss—with the blinds open and the stalker set to show up anytime. They might not have forgotten that if they'd been sober. They might not have done a lot of things if they'd been sober.

Drinking and Thinking

Alcohol and good decisions don't usually go together.

Hannah's the one who brings up the idea of liquid courage. Mixing a little bit of this and a little bit of that, so her parents won't notice any missing alcohol, was something she and Kat used to do. So, nothing new for Hannah.

I'm thinking if she'd skipped those "suicides" she made for her and Courtney, the night might've ended differently. Sober, they probably wouldn't have strayed so far off plan. They would've stayed focused on catching the stalker instead of on daring each other to push personal limits.

Liquid courage gave Courtney the freedom to be what she wanted to be in the moment—attracted to other girls. It gave Hannah permission to do something she wouldn't have normally done—accept Courtney's dare to kiss her. The idea of pushing limits in social norms, common sense, sex, and even safety has been trending for a while. It's not something to brag on. Sometimes, it's just plain stupid. Boundaries exist for a reason. Especially the ones you've set up for yourself. Before you start rushing past the lines of what your gut's telling you, consider the consequences. Think the whole thing through. And if you can't because you're drunk, go to someone you trust. Better yet, don't get drunk.

People make bad choices when they're drunk. Sometimes nothing happens. Other times terrible things happen. Sometimes your no becomes yes by default. You do things you never in a million years would even consider doing. You take chances. Did you know that a lot of risky behavior is alcohol fueled? It's not a surprise really. When you're drunk, the logic and reason part of your brain powers down. You can't process the way you would if you were sober.

And if you're counting on your friends to "take care of you" when you can't take care of yourself, make sure you put that trust in someone who's 100% trustworthy. There are many people who will take advantage. Jessica learned that very hard lesson. She trusted Justin to keep her safe—and he didn't. And now she has to live with the consequences of Bryce's decision to hurt her. But, like I said before, more on that later.

A Violation of Privacy

Rewind to Hannah's room and that kiss. Kissing is intimate. So is taking off your clothes. Neither are casual. Like meeting Justin alone at the park, Hannah rushed into things with Courtney without much thought about what could happen next. And what happens next is that Tyler shows up and takes pictures of them kissing in a huge violation of their privacy, which neither of them did anything about.

What Courtney did do was betray Hannah. Not right away though. First she decides to pretend nothing happened. The morning after Tyler took the picture, Hannah waits for Courtney before school to talk about the night before, only to be blown off and told that everything's fine.

But then, courtesy of a group text from Tyler, one of the pictures makes its way through the school. Unable to stay buried in denial, Courtney finds Hannah at her locker and blames her for what happened. "You of all people should know what a picture can do to a person's life." Wow. No wonder Hannah said, "Girls are evil."

Cue radio silence for the next few weeks until Hannah can't take it anymore. Approaching Courtney in the lunchroom, she points out that both need a friend. Someone who won't judge them. Courtney's other friends show up, and Hannah gets talked into driving them all to the Winter Ball.

At the dance, Bryce flashes the picture and tells Courtney and Hannah he knows it's them. She sidesteps with an insult and pulls Courtney away. But then Monty makes a move on Courtney on the dance floor, suggesting maybe she and Hannah are up for some fun later. Courtney freaks out, terrified someone will discover her secret sexuality.

To deflect, she lies and says it's Laura and Hannah. To sell the lie, she says Hannah asked her to join in a three way, confirms the rumors about Justin getting to third base with Hannah, and throws in that Hannah returned the favor. Monty shares all this with Hannah in front of Clay. Courtney's betrayal kicks off a round of new rumors that leaves Hannah completely humiliated. And who wouldn't be? She trusted Courtney, and Courtney stabbed her in the back.

Humiliation Isn't Fatal

Humiliation hurts. It can be horrible times a million. Terrible to the thousandth degree. One of the most painful and worst feelings you'll ever have. It leaves us desperate to crawl into a hole and become invisible. It's isolating and lonely. There's no doubt that it can make us feel as though we want to die. I've been there. I'm not trying to downplay anything that happened to Hannah or anything that's happened to you. But humiliation doesn't kill you.

It's not a heart attack or a car wreck or cancer. Humiliation by itself isn't fatal. What can be fatal is what you choose to do about it. What Hannah chose to do about it.

Let it Go

Sometimes being humiliated is a brief incident you get over quickly. Other times it's a major incident that makes you feel like you'll never move on. But trust me—and please hear this—you will. A moment in time, even one that seems to follow you everywhere, is still just a moment. And that moment doesn't define you. You don't have to let it plaster itself to you permanently. You don't have control over what's already happened. You do have control over how you decide to handle it. And you get to decide.

Remember when we talked about the big picture perspective? Here's where it comes in. It's how you look at things that helps you move forward. It's each step you take in the right direction that eventually leaves that moment in the dust. Like the song from *Frozen*, sometimes you just have to let it go.

Back to You, Hannah

Courtney is manipulative. I wouldn't trust her. Unlike her "nice" outside image, inside she's self-serving and cares way too much what other people think. Even after Hannah's death, Courtney's in so much denial over being gay, she tells everyone, "Hannah's truth is not my truth." At the very end, because the tapes are going to be out there, she does finally tell her dad about what happened that night between her and Hannah.

Hannah didn't realize who Courtney really was until it was too late. In her defense, Clay didn't realize it either until after he heard the tape.

It's too bad Hannah didn't let it go the first time Courtney shrugged her off after the kiss. A real friend is willing to talk about issues between you instead of pretending they don't exist. Reaching out again only got Hannah used—for a ride to the dance and as she put it, "Courtney's shield."

After Hannah agrees to drive to the dance, she asks her parents to spring for a limo, justifying it with, "I'm trying to have friends." Her mom's right when she says true friends won't like you or dislike you for a car. Had Hannah put that to the test, she might've realized sooner the kind of person Courtney was. If she and her friends still wanted to go to the dance with Hannah if she didn't drive them, it would've been an assurance that they liked *her*. If they didn't, it would've been her clue that they were just using her. Which, duh, they were.

But here's the thing. Hannah already knew that. So desperate not to be alone, she just couldn't seem to walk away. Her response to her mom about real friends disliking you over a car is, "It's high school. Of course they will." Desperate people make desperate choices. They forget boundaries and forget to protect themselves.

You don't have to be everybody's friend. You're allowed to opt out, and so are they. It's okay to avoid someone you don't trust or walk away from someone who betrays your trust. Don't stay in toxic relationships. Plug your energy in elsewhere. Grieve the loss and move on. One moment in time doesn't define you. Neither do people's words and actions and opinions. Friendships don't either.

It's too bad Hannah didn't see that.

Fonda L. Hart

CHAPTER 6
MARCUS COLE

"Maybe none of us can say who we truly are."

~ Hannah Baker

Marcus is on the honor board. Marcus is the student body president. Marcus is someone teachers respect. Marcus is the guy others follow. He comes across as chill and fun but also uber responsible and even wise.

But that's all just a façade. Because underneath that pretty picture he's painted of who he is, he's all about himself. He even tells Bryce, the captain of the football team, in the locker room, "The rules are different for us."

Authenticity

Authenticity is "being real." Being the same person on the inside as you are on the outside. Something interesting happens when we're with a person who's not authentic. Our brain stands a little more at attention. We aren't always even aware of it. Here's why. Remember the phrase "a wolf in sheep's clothing"? Someone may look more sheep than wolf, however our gut seems to know when that isn't quite true.

I see Marcus as inauthentic. He's not an all-out wolf, but he sure isn't a sheep either. His problem is that he wants people to see him as one person when he's nothing like that person. Like with Courtney, image is everything.

After asking Hannah out on a Dollar Valentine Date, Marcus leaves her hanging. If you've ever been left waiting, wondering if you've been stood up, you know the humiliation.

Sexual Harassment

When Marcus shows an hour late—after Hannah texts him—he doesn't come alone. He brings his buddies along. They take over a table nearby while he sits across from Hannah, who's mad and rightly so. But then he apologizes and jokes around with her just enough to get her to let her guard down. That's when he slides into her side of the booth, tells her his parents are out of town, and suggestively touches her thigh. Almost before she can react, he moves his hand farther up her skirt—where he was never invited—and grins over his shoulder at his friends.

Hannah does the right thing. She pushes him away and yells at him to get off. And Marcus's response? "No sweat. I thought you were easy."

What a huge jerk. Clearly not interested in her as a person or as a girlfriend, Marcus wants to use her to impress Bryce and the guys. That shakes Hannah up. "I couldn't even move. I couldn't even get up or scream." Any girl would be shaken by the incident. Especially if the person assaulting her was someone she thought was a friend. Because when it's your friend, it's more than disrespect. It's a betrayal.

What Marcus does to Hannah is inappropriate on every level. And, by legal definition, is sexual harassment. Yep. There's that term again. And you already know how I feel about that. People need to be held accountable for their actions or they're going to keep hurting you or someone else.

Integrity

Guys like Marcus will sacrifice anything and anyone to preserve a certain image. That includes you. That's because he doesn't have any integrity. The word integrity comes from the Latin adjective "integer," meaning whole or complete.

I like to think of integrity this way. Who you are in the dark—when no one's shining a spotlight on you—is who you really are. Period. What you say and do and even think when no one's watching is the real you.

When someone pretends to be one thing and you find out they're another, keep a distance. They'll always do what's best for them. Find people who do the right thing no matter who's watching or not watching. Those people respect themselves, which means they'll respect you.

You might know, in your head, that someone like Marcus isn't worth your time and emotional energy. But do you believe it enough to act on it and stay away? The ability to keep your head up and hold onto your dignity is priceless—because you are priceless. Yep. You really are.

R-E-S-P-E-C-T

When I think about the word respect, I hear Aretha Franklin belting it out in my head. R.E.S.P.E.C.T. Go listen to it on your phone. That's some power right there.

When Marcus bails on Hannah, she decides to give him "one more chance" and texts him. Stupid Hannah. Her words not mine. When the guys are watching Marcus make his play at the diner, Zach doesn't get why Hannah's even still there after an hour. The guys laugh and clear that right up. If a girl's still hanging around waiting for you, she's there because she wants to hook up. End of story. She doesn't have boundaries. She doesn't respect herself. Therefore, you don't have to respect her either.

Don't put up with a guy who doesn't treat you right. If you let a guy walk all over you, you give the impression that you don't value yourself and that it's okay for him not to value you either. That may not be how you feel, but it's the message you're sending. Guys who don't respect girls take advantage of them, not just physically but emotionally as well. And that's destructive.

Back to You, Hannah

I know I'm repeating myself, but Hannah could've told her parents, called the police, come up with a plan or even taken self-defense to feel more in control and to prepare herself for a next time. And unfortunately, because of Bryce, there was a next time.

She could've reminded herself that it was Marcus, not her, who was in the wrong. She could've been angry at him without allowing what he did to define who she was and make her feel like a victim. Or a slut. And honestly, she could have gotten up and left when he still hadn't shown up 20 minutes late. 20 minutes is plenty of time to wait for someone.

Justin. Tyler. Marcus. If Hannah had held just one of these guys accountable, the others would've thought twice about messing with her. No one wants the police to come knocking on their door. No one wants to go to jail. And taking action and standing up for herself would have made it undeniably clear that she wasn't "easy" like Marcus thought. That might've changed everything down the road with Bryce.

Some of these options might not have helped. But any of them would've been better than the option Hannah chose. Marcus was not worth her taking her life. No guy is worth it no matter what he's done to you. Yeah, whatever you're thinking, that's not worth it either. If you're still alive, there is hope for you. And hope can help you overcome anything.

FONDA L. HART

CHAPTER 7
ZACH DEMPSEY

"I needed you to be a lifeline."
~ Hannah Baker

Zach seems to genuinely care about other people, including Hannah. He's sweet and a little naive, especially compared to the guys he hangs out with. But sometimes his emotions get in his way. When he gets hurt, he lashes out. When it came to Hannah, he could've handled things differently. But what went wrong between them is not all on him. They were a head-spinning pair from the start.

After Marcus sexually harasses Hannah at the diner, Zach consoles her. Reasonably upset over the way Marcus treated her, she unreasonably takes it out on Zach, ignoring his efforts to make her feel better. He tells her he doesn't believe she was there to hook up with Marcus or that shes' easy. I think he really likes her. In fact, before he leaves, he even offers to pay her bill.

The next day, he comes up to her in the cafeteria and tells her that he'd wanted her to be his Dollar Valentine. Suspicious after Marcus, she asks Zach if he was "dared" to talk to her. Which is not completely out there. She's lost her trust in guys and can't tell who wants to use her and who doesn't, which just makes the extreme loneliness she's already feeling so much worse. But instead of walking away, she decides to yell at him in front of everyone in the cafeteria.

What if she had said, "Look. I'm not easy. The rumors aren't true. We won't be doing anything physical. So, if you want to get to know me, you just need to know that up front. We can start with a friendship." If Zach really liked her, he would be happy to start with friendship. If he was toying with her, he wouldn't stick around with those boundaries. That would be the litmus test and a safeguard for her.

Double Standards

On the tape, Hannah says, "You said something stupid. I yelled at you. Big deal. You should have let it go." Wait. Stop. Hold everything. *Did* Zach say something stupid? He'd just taken a risk and told Hannah that while other guys like her for her body parts, "I like you for so much more." Was that a stupid thing to say? I don't think so. Most girls would appreciate someone who likes "so much more" than her looks. Zach meant it as a compliment. A way to say that he liked her for who she was. Hackles already up, Hannah couldn't see it that way, called him an idiot, and told him to leave her alone.

But let's run with Hannah's accusation for a minute and assume what Zach said *was* stupid. To Hannah, saying something stupid is a huge deal. However, what she did when she yelled at him in front of an audience wasn't a big deal. In other words, yelling at someone is nothing. Saying something stupid is everything. Everything wrong that is. What if Hannah said something stupid and someone yelled at her? Would she have let it go the way she told Zach to let it go? I doubt it. That seems a double standard to me.

Stuck on the Roller Coaster

By yelling at Zach, Hannah not only humiliates him, she hurts his feelings. He basically tells her he likes her, and she more or less kicks him where it hurts. Choosing to channel anger over his other emotions—remember we talked about how anger makes us feel powerful instead of vulnerable—he "kicks" her right back when he says, "This s&%$ that happens to you, I think some of it you bring on yourself."

If we're being honest, he's not completely wrong. Except he could've said it in a different way. I do want to point out that when the guys ask him why he would even try with "that girl," he refuses to feed the Hannah hate fest.

Right around this time, Mrs. Bradley sets up compliment bags for each student in Peer Communications where others can leave notes of encouragement. They clearly mean a lot to Hannah. "These are the stupidest, most embarrassing things that I check every day."

And Zach being Zach lets his emotions get in the way of his better judgment and steals the notes from Hannah's bag, unknowingly taking away one of the only things Hannah feels she has left. She equates it to cutting her lifeline because, "Sometimes the little things mean more than anyone knows." She then writes a super personal letter about how lonely and isolated she feels and sticks it into her bag for him to find.

Here's where things get interesting. Hannah claimed Zach crumpled that letter and threw it on the ground, making him appear coldhearted. Only later, after her death, he shows it to Clay and offers to let him read it. Huh. Now I'm wondering how much of what Hannah said in those tapes was truly accurate. Some people believed Hannah's truth was the truth. Other's didn't. But a few of them had their own reasons for calling her a liar.

Moving on in the Zach/Hannah roller coaster. Isn't it a little odd how she calls him out in one moment and bares her soul to him in the next? And why did she give him that letter? That kind of letter isn't something you give to just anyone. Her emotions, especially her suicidal thoughts, were not Zach's responsibility and would overwhelm any teenager—and a lot of adults too.

Some people think sharing something intense with the person they like will make that person fall for them. I'm not just talking about girls. Guys can be "dudes in distress" as much as girls can be "damsels in distress." Both are looking for a hero/heroine to step in and rescue them.

Expecting someone to rescue you—especially someone you're not already in a close relationship with—is a setup for disappointment. It's also unhealthy and kind of selfish. On the other side of it, a person willing to jump into the "deep end" with you right away is probably also emotionally unhealthy.

Anonymous for All to See

"What if the only way to stop feeling bad is to stop feeling anything at all forever?" When Mrs. Bradley reads that off a Monet's napkin from the anonymous question bag, everyone thinks Skye wrote it because she works there. And outwardly, she fits the bill. I find it interesting that she doesn't deny it. She knew Hannah wrote it—she saw her writing on the napkin. Does she keep that to herself because she doesn't care what people think of her or because she's trying to respect Hannah's privacy? I think it's a little of both. We do know she takes the question seriously when she says, "It's not a joke," after someone mentioned it might be.

As Mrs. Bradley continues the discussion, Hannah looks at Zach—who looks away—as if she wants him to out her as the author. To speak for her when she can't. She later says, "You had to know I wrote that note." Maybe he did, but he was trying to avoid getting caught in the crossfire of her drama or trying to respect her privacy like Skye. Or maybe he didn't know. Undoubtedly, he couldn't read Hannah's mind the way she expected.

Whatever his reason, Hannah gets upset at him. But if she wanted people to know those were her feelings, wasn't it then it her responsibility to share them?

Great Expectations

Do you see a pattern? She tells Justin he was her *kryptonite*. She tells Alex he became her *hurricane*. She tells Zach he failed to be her *lifeline*. That's intense! Like Zach told Clay, "Hannah was too much." She'd only known each of these guys for a short time when she set these expectations. I'm guessing that if any of them had even guessed what she wanted from them, they'd have ghosted her right up front.

Here's a reality check. No one person can meet all your needs. No sane seventeen-year-old is even going to try. It's not realistic to hand over so much power, responsibility, and vulnerability to someone else. That kind of thing doesn't come with a happy ending. Either the other person will run scared and let you down, or they'll take advantage of you. It's also a big, big boundary violation. Hannah violated Zach's boundaries by dumping that letter on him. But she violated her own by sharing the deepest parts of her heart when she needed to be protecting them.

Locus of Control

Sounds a little weird, huh? Simply put, your "locus of control" is the part of you that helps you figure out what you can and can't control in life. For example, you can't control what time the sun comes up. But you can control what time you wake up by setting your alarm.

Your locus of control is either internal or external. Which one depends on how you see things. It's internal if you believe there are things in life you can control and that you have the power to make positive things happen. It's external when you believe there aren't things in life you can control and that you don't have the power to make positive things happen.

Think of it like a video game controller that moves you left or right or up or down or forward or backward in the game of life. Are you in charge of your own controller or is some outside force?

It's important to realize that people who give that controller away, people with an external locus of control, believe that life just happens to them. They won't even try to make positive changes because they don't even see that as a possibility. They're fatalistic.

Internal Locus of Control

Let's say you hate taking the bus to school, but you don't have a car. You decide to get a job to save up for one. You make sure to be on time for work. Work hard. Be responsible. Get along with others. Put aside a big chunk of every paycheck. And save up for insurance too. You do all of this because you want your own car. And *you* are able to make it happen. Bye-bye bus. Hello freedom.

In this situation, you're operating from an internal locus of control. You choose to make things happen.

External Locus of Control

This time you're in this same situation, but you spend your energy wishing you had a car or rich parents or better luck. You resent or envy those who do have a car but don't do anything to get one yourself. You spend your time dwelling on the idea that life sucks and if you just had a car—or insert whatever you think you want that will make things better here—life would be great. Here you're operating from an external locus of control.

In both examples, you want the same thing and have the same circumstances. Only in the first, you take steps and make sacrifices to go after what you want and make life better. In the second, you continue as is, doing nothing to move forward, and you have to take the bus. Life works better when you have an internal locus of control that empowers you to grab that video game controller and take charge.

So, what *can* you control? What can you *not* control? You know this one. You don't have control over what other people do. But you do have control over what you do and how you respond.

Back to You, Hannah

Hannah plays with having an internal locus of control. Sort of. The summer before junior year, she wants a fresh start and decides to push the "reset button" on her life. Part of that fresh start is to stop partying and be more disciplined. But then the first party rolls around. "There I was, the new me, doing the same old things."

Hannah had some good intentions. And . . . good intentions alone don't make positive things happen or keep negative things from happening. She didn't take charge and go after what she wanted. She put too many expectations on other people to save her while she stood by and let the chips fall. Here's a few examples of what Hannah believed versus the actual truth.

Hannah said:
- (about college) "If you don't have the money, and don't have the brains, your decisions are made for you."

The Truth: Hannah wanted to go to college. She hadn't taken the SAT or the ACT, and her GPA wasn't high enough to qualify for financial aid. But she still had time. She could've invested in studying for those tests and working harder to get her grades up. She had two years left to change the course of her future. Instead, she just gave up.

- (about being labeled a slut) "It gets posted, and you become that girl."

The Truth: You either are that girl or you aren't. Someone posting it doesn't make it true. Definition time. A slut is someone who has multiple casual sex partners. If you do, then by definition you are. If you don't, then by definition you aren't. You are 100% in control of that process. It has nothing to do with what gets posted. What people say about you does not define you. Hannah didn't have to "become that girl." And neither do you.

- (about being lonely) "Humans are a social species. We rely on connection . . . I'm quoting from a school textbook. Too bad nobody bothered to read it."

The Truth: Hannah had no way of knowing who read that textbook and who didn't. It's a bizarre assumption. It's equally strange that she somehow connected this idea with her loneliness. As if other people would somehow mysteriously know how lonely she was and do something about it—without her saying anything. Without her taking responsibility for her own feelings and needs. Life doesn't work like that. Neither do people. If Hannah had let the people who cared about her, like Clay, know she was lonely, that might've changed.

- (about what boys say to girls) "That's how it works in high school. Boys talk. Girls listen."

The Truth: I'm gonna cheat here a bit. It's true, some boys do a lot of talking. And some girls will listen and not talk, especially if they're crushing on a guy. But there's no rule that it has to be that way. For girls, this is part of learning to assert themselves and even to have the courage to respectfully disagree. In the 21st Century, it's a level playing field and girls can talk. Some boys even like to listen. Just boundary it, ladies. Don't tell him every detail of every aspect of your life. Guaranteed, he'll gloss over and stop listening. But then again, you'd probably do the same to him.

I think you get the idea. Hannah had the power to make life better for *herself*. But she didn't take it. Had she grabbed what was hers to control, her life could've been—would've been—so different. I believe she'd still be alive. Maybe she'd even be happy.

HEALTHY RELATIONSHIPS

Let's talk a little bit about what goes into healthy relationships. I've mentioned them in other chapters, and I'll mention them again. They're more important than you think. Just one strong connection with someone else can change the way you feel about yourself—be it positive or negative.

When our relationships are good for us and help us feel connected and safe, it's easy to feel good about life. When our relationships aren't good for us and make us feel disconnected, isolated, or stuck, it's hard to feel good about life. Whether we're struggling with bad relationships or the lack of relationships, our hearts are heavy, we feel lonely, and everything takes more effort.

Romance

Since romance is where a lot of people look for connection, we'll start with that. Whether you're committed to a person, committed to the sex, or just playing around, what you keep or give away physically and emotionally affects how you see yourself.

Dating Around

I had a conversation with a seventeen-year-old guy recently. He said he's not interested in doing the one-person thing at the moment and wants to play the field. But he feels guilty. Confused about his guilt, I explained to him that dating around and talking to different people is a great idea and a good way to figure out what you like in a person. It also gives you an opportunity to figure out who you are as a single person before you get locked into being the other half of a couple. So many people can lose themselves and their identities when they rush into and stay in a long-term relationship when they're young. There's no need to hurry. There's plenty of time for that kind of intense relationship later.

The very next day I had a conversation with a fifteen-year-old girl about the very same thing. She explained that when people "date around," they don't actually go on dates—they just message each other and say things they don't mean or shouldn't be saying. They may flirt with or sext with different people and even throw out "I love you" to several at a time. And they're not serious about any of them. Okay, that's not "dating around." It's not even dating! You can't really believe anything a person says in those situations. The words are empty and meaningless. And everyone knows it. So why bother doing it?

The healthy version of dating around, that lets you figure out what kind of person you ultimately want to be with and what kind of person you are, involves actual dates—meaning you hang out with numerous people and get to know them face to face without crossing lines sexually. There's no expectation of it going beyond casual encounters unless you both decide to be exclusive with each other. Dating around keeps it light and helps you not say things you don't mean. You respect each other's dignity and feelings and don't play games. It's a short-term process that keeps the long view in mind.

Modest Is Hottest

On a side note, you might be surprised to know that guys do find modest girls attractive. Nothing says you have to put it all out there for everyone to see. There's something to be said for leaving what's under your clothes to the imagination. Why not stand out by being different? You don't need to be sexy for the whole world—just for your own man. Guys who respect girls are attracted to girls who like themselves and who hold onto their dignity. And here's something you might not have thought of. Most guys will treat a girl as well as she expects to be treated. Set the bar higher. You deserve the best.

Being One on One

You like a guy. He seems to like you. You're spending some time together, and he wants to be exclusive. Cool! Except, before long, he wants to start having sex. Maybe not so cool.

What if you don't want to go there but you're afraid you'll lose him if you don't? You just found him. You don't want him to leave and find someone else. But how do you know whether he's into you or whether he's just into your body? Once you sleep with him, you'll have no way of knowing.

Let's break this down.

If you say no, and he sticks around, it's probably because he really likes and is genuinely interested in *you*. He's still physically drawn to you, of course. That's the power of testosterone. But because he wants to be with *you*, he respects your boundaries. It feels special to be liked for who you are and not for what he can get from you, doesn't it? When you hold onto your values, you'll like and respect yourself and him. That's a pretty good feeling. And bonus—you'll trust him more.

If you say no, and he goes somewhere else, well, there's your answer. It's not you he wants, it's sex. You may be sad that he moved on. But be glad you didn't give it up for someone who isn't really committed to you. Disappointing as it is, it will save you heartbreak and regret further down the line. I'll take disappointment over heartbreak any day.

If you say yes too soon, it will hard be to tell if he cares about *you* beyond that. When you're together, you'll never quite be sure if he's all about spending time with *you* or your body. Once you bring sex into a relationship, it makes things so much more complicated. And the focus of who you are as a couple tends to change. This is why girls who give in to sex when they're not ready tend to be less secure and more clingy. They never really know where they stand. And wondering why someone likes you and if they're only using you is a stressful way to relationship.

Girls who respect themselves seem to have a much easier time saying no. A girl who doesn't, for whatever reason, is usually more likely to say yes. She believes she's not good enough to be liked or loved or will do whatever a guy asks to keep his interest. Being liked is more important to her than protecting herself and her feelings.

She's allowing her worth on being wanted to be mirrored by someone who might not even be worthy of her anyway. Do you know what you're worth? Do you know what makes you beautiful—especially on the inside? I do. It's your personality, your character, and the way you treat people. That's what makes you attractive and fun to be around. That's what draws a guy in. And if he doesn't care about those things, he's not worth your time. Please know that and believe it.

By the way ladies, if a guy talks a lot about how well he treats girls, he probably doesn't. Guys who genuinely respect girls and treat them well do so because it's who they are. It doesn't occur to them to brag about it. It's just part of their character.

To Sex or Not to Sex

So, what are the rules of engagement in a relationship when it comes to sex? I'm all about timeless truth. And one timeless truth is this—morality is practical. I figure if it's been around for thousands of years, it must be worth looking at.

- Here are some timeless truths to hold onto:
- you're never obligated to have sex with anyone ever
- you're not responsible to satisfy someone else's physical needs
- you don't owe a guy anything
- you don't need a reason or an excuse
- "no" is a complete sentence
- Here are some reasons to say no:
- if you feel uneasy or uncomfortable

- if you don't feel physically or emotionally safe
- if it's not what you want right now—even if it has been what you've wanted before
- if you simply don't want to
- if your "gut" says no
- If your heart says no
- if your conscience will bother you after
- if you have second thoughts
- if it doesn't feel "right"
- if you aren't completely sure
- if you're being pressured
- if you're being hurt or abused
- if you're saving yourself for someone else

Feel free to add to this list. Any one reason is reason enough. Sex is more than a few moments of physical closeness. Whether you want the feelings that come with it or not, the lasting emotions can be intense. Don't set yourself up for regrets.

Very few girls who lose their virginity in their teens are glad they had sex when they did. Most wish they would've waited. You're more likely to regret having said yes than having said no. You're more likely to have more sexual partners once you start. Once you've gone there, you can't go back. And each person you do it with makes it less and less special. This is one area where it's always good to keep the big picture. You can always decide to have sex later. But you can't take it back once you have.

Friendships

Being isolated leads to loneliness, anxiety, and depression. People weren't designed to do life by themselves. While there are many different types of relationships we can have, friendship is one of the best. True friendship, anyway. But not all friendships are equal. Sometimes what we see as friendship isn't that at all.

Fake Friendships

There are two kinds of fake friends—opportunists and users.

I don't mean opportunists in the sense that these people are hanging around waiting to take advantage of you. I mean it in the sense that they're comrades of convenience. They're not looking for friendship, but hey, life threw you together and made the "friendship" easily accessible.

You meet at work or school or on a team or where you live. They have to be there. You have to be there. They're okay. You're okay. You have one or two things in common. You might study together, take work breaks together, or just hang out. You might even share parts of yourself with each other. But when circumstances stop putting you together, one or both of you move on. A young adult I know termed them "millennial friendships." When the convenience is gone, so are they. The friendship is completely expendable. And that's because nothing of value was put into it.

Users on the other hand want something from you—who you know, your money, your ride, even your blind admiration. Some people work hard to collect their own fan club. It's all about what *you* can do for *them*. It might seem like they're giving back, but if you look hard enough, the illusion will fall away. And so will they once you've lost your value. A true friendship is about both people.

Destructive Friendships

This type of friend can be a user as well. But they're more dangerous. And usually better at hiding the truth of your relationship and the truth of who they are. This is the kind of friendship that makes you go against your values, your boundaries, and the core of who you are.

Some destructive friendships are based in control and mind games. Like the friend who manipulates you into doing what they want using persuasion or fear. Or the friend who puts you on a pedestal and compliments you . . . then shreds you verbally. You never know quite what to expect from these kinds of people. They keep you guessing—in the worst way.

It can also be the friend who threatens to hurt themselves if you don't jump to their demands or betray your trust and share your secrets if you hold to your boundaries. By the way, these kinds of threats have another name—emotional blackmail.

So, what are some ways to tell if your relationship is healthy or not? You might be in a destructive relationship if:

- the other people in your life don't like your friend
- you feel pressured to violate your own values and boundaries
- you have to keep saying no
- you dread spending time together
- you feel obligated to the friendship
- you're expected to rescue someone else

But the biggest clue is . . . you. If someone brings out the worst in you, the friendship isn't healthy. A healthy relationship brings out the best in you and even makes you a better person, if you're open to growing. And a healthy relationship doesn't have to be hidden from your friends and family.

In a true friendship, where both people value each other, you should never have to go against your beliefs, repeatedly say no, hang out when you feel uncomfortable, feel forced to stay, or be expected to be someone's savior.

Genuine Friendships

Friendship can sometimes seem complicated. But it doesn't have to be. Honesty is key. When both people are being real—and trust and respect are at the center of the relationship—it's entirely possible to have "life-giving" friendships. But that's up to both of you. Friendship goes both ways. We choose how we treat those we call friends, and they chose how they treat us.

You've probably seen cliches about friendship like, "Friends are the flowers in the garden of life." Cheesy, right? But when you think about it, there are numerous parallels between friendship and a garden. Growing vibrant, fragrant flowers requires healthy soil, adequate sunshine, enough water, and occasional pruning. Ouch! Did you know that when you prune a plant properly, it produces more and larger flowers?

Friendship is the same. Being able to weather storms and grow together is part of what deepens a friendship. Only here, the soil is trust. The sun is sharing good times. Fun and laughter make good memories. I call those good memories "cup-filling" times because everybody involved hopefully comes away feeling like their "cup" is full. The water is supporting each other through the good and the bad. And pruning is honest but kind feedback—sometimes telling each other things that aren't always pleasant to hear. But that's where the other person brings out the best in us. Genuine pruning is healthy. Tearing each other down is not.

When you invest positive things into someone and choose people who do the same, your proverbial "garden" of friendship will become a safe place where you'll want to be. But watch out for the "weeds" that can spoil your garden—competition, jealousy, gossip, betrayal, and lies. True friends celebrate each other's successes and are genuinely happy for each other. They don't talk behind each other's backs. That's a violation of trust that "drains the cup."

If something is bothering you, respect your friend and yourself by telling them directly. Did you know that miscommunication and misunderstanding are some of the top reasons friendships fail? True friends can tell each other how they feel, what they need, and trust that they will be heard. Just be careful to say something the way you would want to hear it. Leaving things unsaid dries up the trust in your friendship, and nothing can bloom where trust is lacking. And always, always be willing to say "I'm sorry" when you mess up. A good friendship has no place for stubborn pride.

Parents—Can't Live With 'em, Can't Live Without 'em

Anyone have a mom or dad whose favorite word seems to be no? How many times have you been frustrated when your parents nixed something you thought was perfectly reasonable? You might think they're being ridiculous and overly worried about nothing. But what if their goal is to protect you from things that could go wrong? Believe it not, they have life experience that you don't and sometimes see "red flags" you might miss.

You might think you already know a lot about life. And compared to five years ago when you were younger, you do. You can probably see that if you have a younger sister or brother. But just imagine how much more you'll know in five or ten more years. It just makes sense that more years equal more experience.

Not everyone is lucky enough to have parents who genuinely care. If you have parents who are interested, be happy—even if they're a little "helicoptery." Don't waste that resource. Use it to your advantage. Old people weren't always old, you know—and they aren't completely clueless. They were young once with parents of their own, having some of the same thoughts you're having now.

Yes, your "growing up world" is very different than mine. I won't even pretend it isn't extremely complicated. Thanks to social media, the issues and struggles you're navigating bring a whole new set of obstacles and consequences. Facebook. Twitter. Instagram. They sure intensify the peer pressure, don't they?

But even if people older than you didn't walk those things out in their teen years, they did face many of the same feelings. And speaking as one of those people, most of us want to help. Even if it's just to be your cheerleader when everyone else has left you in the dust. Before you shut your parents out, why don't you give them a chance to hold you up when you're ready to fall and see what happens. Take a chance. You might be glad you did.

Trust and Trustability

Let's talk about trust—the foundation of any relationship. What are some traits of a person who is trustworthy? Bottom line, they keep their word. When they say yes, they mean yes. When they say no, they mean no. Here are some questions that apply to every relationship.

Do I trust you?
Are you trustworthy?
Do you trust me?
Am I trustworthy?

Don't you hate it when someone says they're going to do something or be somewhere and don't follow through? You're left hanging and confused about what's going on. Did his car break down? Did he forget about you? Does she not care? Did she not know how to say no and just decide not to show up?

If someone lets you down once or twice but usually come through, you may want to give them the benefit of the doubt. If they have a track record of flaking or not taking you seriously, it may be time to rethink the relationship and who you put your trust in.

Remember what we talked about in Mirror, Mirror? When someone repeatedly can't be counted on, it's easy to start seeing that as a reflection of your worth when it's really a reflection of them. If you know your worth, it's easier to top wasting your time on someone who's not trustworthy.

Sometimes I hear people say that they got hurt and will never trust anyone again. That's tragic. If you've chosen not to trust *anyone ever*, you're missing out on one of life's most special experiences. Even in good relationships, people sometimes hurt each other. There's no way to completely avoid that.

We all want to be seen for who we are. It's frustrating when someone thinks they know you, but they're off target. When the things they believe about you are not only untrue but don't even come close to who you really are. It's painful to be accused when we are innocent.

If you're putting a lot of effort into trying to get someone to trust you, you leave yourself open to being manipulated and controlled. Especially if the goalpost keeps getting moved further and further down the field in terms of what that person expects from you. How do you decide how far you'll go and how long you'll keep trying to do the impossible before you stop taking responsibility for someone else's lack of trust? There's a difference between being trustworthy and having to constantly prove you can be trusted.

We talked about people's "yes" and "no" earlier. Those willing to say no are usually seen as more trustworthy. They don't just say yes to placate others. Even if you're disappointed with their "no," at least you know what to expect. You don't feel disrespected or devalued. Someone who says no respects you enough not to string you along.

You're never obligated to be in a relationship. If you feel like you're in an unhealthy one, walk away. Decide this is not a person you want in your life. Seriously. You don't even need to give them a reason. Just leave. Quit watering toxic romances or friendships. Because nobody intentionally waters weeds, right?

CHAPTER 8
RYAN SHAVER

"Liberty High's resident intellectual. Editor of Lost and Found. General selfish snob."
~ Hannah Baker

Artist. Poet. Boundary violator. Jerk. Creative thinkers like Ryan often live by a different set of boundaries. Or no boundaries. And if you haven't already noticed, Ryan doesn't have a lot of redeemable qualities. Even Tony, who dated him, said Ryan was "serious about the 'zine, his shoes, and not much else."

Poetic License

Like Justin—with Bryce as an accomplice—and Tyler, Ryan invades Hannah's privacy, takes something personal of hers, and puts it out there for everyone to see. Only he uses the idea of poetic license to make it "okay." It isn't.

During her "Ryan period," Hannah is looking for purpose. "A reason for being on this planet." When she's invited to a poetry club by a librarian she meets at college day, she reluctantly checks it out. Ryan is the only person there her age. Moved by his poetry, she asks him to teach her how to write like that—in a way that draws people in and makes them feel what he's feeling—and he does. They spend time together, and it seems like they're building a friendship based on something they have in common.

Assured poetry club is "safe place," Hannah shares a very intimate, soul-baring poem. Impressed by her creativity, Ryan tells her she should publish it. That "people need to see it because it will change them." Hannah tells him absolutely not.

Ignoring her "no," Ryan tears the page out of her journal and publishes it in *Lost and Found*. Can you imagine having something so totally and deeply personal go viral at school? Ugh! It would feel like walking the halls naked. Yes, it was anonymous. But really? It was in her handwriting. And people quickly figured it out.

She's horrified. Wouldn't you be? And he doesn't even regret it! He tells her, "I did you a favor." And tells her that when she looks back on it later, she'll admit he was right. What. A. Grade. A. Jerk.

Back to You, Hannah

After the poem is out there, there is nothing Hannah can do to take it back or take away the humiliation of feeling vulnerable and exposed. She didn't make a bad choice here. Going to the poetry club should've been fine. For the most part, it seemed a safe place. Those people she mentioned that were decades older and looked like they belonged in an AA meeting never would've stolen her poem and used it against her. Grown-ups typically don't treat people that way. If Ryan hadn't been there, her words would've remained hers and hers alone.

Okay, trusting Ryan enough to spend time with him wasn't the best idea. But there's no way she could've known what he was going to do. She didn't hand him the poem and then ask him to keep it "off the record." He took it from her without her consent. It seems people took a lot of things from her without her consent.

In this situation, Hannah's power was in standing up for herself and moving forward. She did the right thing confronting Ryan. In being assertive, we get to use our voice, be heard, and set a different course. We show the person who took advantage of us or betrayed us that they can't walk all over us. Sometimes there are things you have no control over. Your control lies in how you handle them. I'm not saying it's not hard. What Ryan did to Hannah was destructive. But she didn't have to take it on and carry it around.

Sometimes it's worth asking, "How much time and energy is this worth?" What if she'd invested the energy—and face it, hate—that went into making Ryan's tape into figuring out how to get past her embarrassment? There's not one person alive who hasn't been embarrassed badly at least once or twice. And trust me, you'll have plenty more of those moments in life. But nothing is stopping you from holding onto your dignity, keeping your head up, and finding out what you can learn from what happened. If you give yourself a chance, you will get past it. There's a reason why people in AA use this short prayer at the beginning and sometimes the end of every meeting.

The Serenity Prayer

God, grant me the serenity to
> accept the things I cannot change,
> courage to change the things I can,
> and wisdom to know the difference.

For Hannah, what Ryan did—and her reaction to it—was just one more burden added to the heavy pack she already carried. One more step forward on that path to make the pain stop. One more off-ramp she could have taken but didn't.

CHAPTER 9
JUSTIN (again)

"And people don't really change."

~ Hannah Baker

On this tape, Hannah says she has three stories to tell about Jessica's party. Like Hannah, we'll talk more about what happened with Sheri in her chapter and what happened between Hannah and Clay in his. But for now, Justin, it's all you. Again.

People are mostly a package deal—the good, the bad, and the otherwise. And Justin is definitely all of those. He can be hard to figure out. On one hand, he comes across as a good guy stuck in a bad situation. On the other, his loyalty to Bryce comes with terrible consequences, things he eventually can't live with. That loyalty sure led to his worst moment—Jessica's rape.

We're doing to dig deep into rape soon. Rape deserves an entire chapter of its own, an entire book of its own really, and some very real discussion. Don't think I'm glossing over Bryce's assault on Jessica. I promise I'm not. There's not enough room to talk about it here. So, for now, Justin's second tape is about Justin, what he did, what he didn't do, and the damage it caused.

Justin and Jessica

Girl meets boy. Boy falls in love with girl. Girl falls in love with boy. Boy gives girl a rose the night of their two-month anniversary. And everything's perfect forever. Right? Wrong. And not just because it's high school and high-school sweethearts who stay together long term are few and far between. For Jessica and Justin, there could never be a happily ever after. Not after what happens at her party.

Jessica starts dating Justin during summer school. After the picture he took of Hannah at the beginning of sophomore year. After Hannah warned her about him way back at the Winter Ball. When it comes to Justin, Jessica doesn't seem super open to advice from her former friend.

But Hannah tries one more time at the party, asking why Jessica's dating him. Still not getting the point, Jessica goes into sarcastic mode. "Do I need your permission?" Then promptly launches into excuses for what he did to Hannah. "You guys weren't even technically dating. Bryce was the one who sent the photo not Justin."

The Party

Pretty much everyone gets drunk that night, including Hannah, Jessica, and Justin. Remember when we talked about thinking and drinking and making bad and good decisions? This applies here more than ever. It's about consequences and personal safety. It would be so awesome to be able to go to a party and not have to think about those things. But that's not reality. Especially if you're a girl. It stinks that I even have to say that.

I'm sure the thought never crosses Jessica's mind that she has to worry about being safe in her own house. Like most teens, she feels a little bit invincible. Like nothing's going to happen to *her*. When Hannah tells her to be careful with Justin, she says, "I'm fine. I know what I'm doing."

And she's right. As far as her line of thinking goes. She doesn't believe Justin's going to take advantage of her. Even Hannah, who's hiding in the room for her own reasons before either of them get there, wants to believe he'll be the "good guy" and let Jessica sleep it off.

I think he would have. Yes, he really wants to mess around with her, and I'm sure he's hoping she'll come around enough to consent. But he also knows they're dating. That they have more than just this night to be alone together. He has plenty of chances to hit her up when she's sober. It's what happens next, when he goes to get her water, that Jessica couldn't foresee.

At this point, Hannah tries to leave, but she doesn't get far. She hears a *thump* out in the hall, and then Bryce comes into the room. Later we see that Justin tried to keep Bryce out, but he pushes Justin out of the way, outright stating, "What's mine is yours." While Justin puts up a small fight, after Bryce locks him out of the room, he gives up. We all know what happens next, and Hannah witnesses every horrible second of it.

If Jessica had a crystal ball to see into the future, I'm certain she wouldn't have gotten drunk or counted on her boyfriend to protect her. Justin probably had no clue he would need to be her protector, or he would've stayed sober and kept her off Bryce's radar. But hindsight can't change anything that's already been done. It can only give you tools to change things up and make better choices going forward. I wish that wasn't true. But it is.

Rape Is Not Your Fault

Here's something you really need to know. Believing it might take time but get it in your head now so you can come to terms with it in your heart later. If you've ever been assaulted or raped, *it was not your fault*.

Not your fault.

No matter what you did or didn't do, it is not your fault. Don't even play that game with yourself. There's nothing a person can do to deserve being raped. *Nothing*. Nope, whatever you're thinking—the answer is, "No not that." And not "that" either. You did not bring it on yourself. Rape is not normal or acceptable in any situation. Under any circumstances. Ever.

Denial

Rape is a type of assault that impacts every part of a person. It's an intrusion of body and soul that devastates us and leaves us extremely messed up. Even if we don't act like it. And that's important to remember.

Deep down, Jessica realizes what happened to her—she sees Bryce in flashbacks—but she buries herself so deep in denial she's left with no choice but to trust in Justin's version of that night.

Because then what happened to her can't be real. And she doesn't have to deal with. It can't touch her. Only it does. It touches her every day.

Without that denial, Jessica would be left to face two things. That Bryce raped her. And that Justin could've stopped it and didn't. That he betrayed her not by what he did but by what he didn't do.

Pretending something didn't happen never makes it go away. It always makes it worse. Jessica needed help. If something like this ever happens to you, you need help too. It's so hard to try and get through something this heavy alone. Don't put that on yourself because you're too scared or too ashamed to admit the truth. What happened to you is not your shame to own.

The Borrowed Emotions of Guilt and Shame

So many people victimized by rape are tormented by guilt and shame—emotions they don't have to take on. Do you know the difference between guilt and shame? Because there is a huge difference.

- Guilt is what you feel when you've done something wrong or chosen not to do something right.
- Shame is the sense that there's something wrong with you—not just your behavior.

Being sexually assaulted is intensely personal and makes you feel vulnerable. But it's not a decision you made or a decision you didn't make. You have nothing to feel guilty about. People are responsible for their own actions. Guilt belongs solely to the rapist. Even if he, like Bryce, won't accept it.

It's natural to feel shame. But what you're feeling is not your shame. Again, shame belongs solely to the rapist. He should feel ashamed of what he is. Even if he doesn't.

Rapists and molesters often will tell their victims that what's happening is their fault. They impose a sense of shame and guilt. Why? To keep their victims quiet—in some cases so they can go on abusing them. Think about it. If you feel guilt and shame over an assault or repeated assaults, you're far less likely to reach out for help. It's an invisible shackle around your neck that keeps you quiet. This is an additional layer of violation.

PTSD

Post-Traumatic Stress Disorder is a mental health condition that starts as a result of trauma—where a person experiences something terrifying or painful and feels like their safety or their life is threatened. Or witnesses someone else's safety or life being threatened.

It is good to know though that just because you experience or witness trauma, it doesn't mean you'll automatically have PTSD. Some people do. Some people don't. And it doesn't have anything to do with how "strong" or "weak" of a person you are. You don't choose it or not choose it. Like when we talked about feelings. Feelings aren't good or bad, they just are. It's the same with PTSD. It just is.

Slowly, over time, Jessica sinks into a downward spiral. You can see it in her appearance before and after Hannah's death. And you can see it in the things she does that are completely out of character. Here are just a few. She skips cheerleading practice, vandalizes the stage at school, comes onto Justin and gets upset when he pushes her away, starts drinking, and goes from someone who cares about her life to someone who doesn't. She even hangs out with Bryce, alone, on purpose.

Even he can tell that something's seriously wrong with her. He doesn't take any of the responsibility for what he did, doesn't even seem to feel the slightest remorse over it, but he sees what's happening to her—going as far as to say, "What are you, insane?" And she answers, "Maybe a little."

But Jessica's not insane. Having Post-Traumatic Stress Disorder does not mean you're crazy. You may *feel* crazy because of the way trauma changes your brain. But based on the horrible thing that happened to you, your reactions are normal. That doesn't mean they're healthy.

Self-Medicating

Trauma can actually rewire your brain, making it almost impossible to be calm or feel peace. With PTSD, you don't get a break from the horrible thing that happened to you.

Let's go back to Jessica's drinking. Yes, she drank before at parties and with other people. But after the rape, she starts drinking alone. All the time. In her room. And at school. While the rape flashes back to her in pieces and she works hard to keep her head buried in the sand, her body knows the truth and keeps score. And her body isn't feeling right. It won't let her forget. At first, she probably doesn't pick up on why she's drinking more. But Justin, who has his own self-medicating issues, sees it's becoming a problem. And so do the people around her.

Many people with PTSD use alcohol, weed, Xanax, or other medications to numb their trauma. And those things help. For a short time. But they come with a very serious side effect—addiction. Yes, even weed can be addictive. Don't listen to your friends on that one. Do your own research.

All those "tools to forget" listed above are called central nervous system depressants. In other words, they slow down your brain and nervous system. They can make you depressed, mess with your ability to concentrate and focus, and slow your reaction time. That's why we keep talking about how it's not safe to drink—or take any of those other things—and then drive. And for you athletes out there, anything that depresses your central nervous system also really screws up your reflexes.

Eventually self-medicating can make you stupid on so many levels. And it cons your body into dependence to the point where you don't feel "right" unless you keep upping how much and how often you use your drug of choice. Alcohol, weed, Xanax, or anything else you take won't heal your brain or help you move forward from your trauma. And over time, you'll become more depressed.

There are healthy ways to move forward. Ways that work. I'm going to share them in the PTSD time-out. Thankfully, Jessica finally decides for herself that enough is enough. She wants something better for her life and is ready to do something to make that happen. She starts by dumping out all the bottles of alcohol hidden under her bed and telling her Dad about the rape.

Justin

Justin has his own self-medicating habits. He tends to get stoned, sometimes for days at a time. First because his mom isn't a mom to him, and he knows he won't ever be able to count on her. It's not a one-off when Seth, her current meth-head boyfriend, chokes Justin who looks to her for help, and she clearly picks boyfriend over son. Yes, she suggests to Seth that if he doesn't let Justin go, the neighbors might call the police. But for real? What kind of a person does that to her child?

Second, Justin gets stoned because he can't handle his part in Jessica's rape or covering up for Bryce afterward. Hannah says, "This tape isn't about him (Bryce). You called him a friend. But your girlfriend needed you." Justin screwed up big time when it came to Jessica.

- strike 1: Justin fails to protect Jessica when she can't protect herself. He knows what Bryce is going to do—he knows Bryce!—and he doesn't do everything in his power to stop it from happening.
- strike 2: He lies about what happened, telling Jessica that they had sex that night. And sticks with that story almost to the end, telling Clay, "We hooked up. She wanted it, and we hooked up."
- strike 3: He talks himself into believing Jessica needs that lie. "I was trying to protect you." To appease his own guilt, he needs to think that if she doesn't know, that if no one knows, she'll be fine.
- strike 4: He stays friends with Bryce and defends that choice. Finally unable to keep what he knows from Jessica any longer, he tells her what really happened—in front of all the guys, including Bryce. The next day, Justin comes to see

Jessica and ends up defending his loyalty to Bryce because Bryce took Justin in when he had nowhere to go, fed him when he was starving, bought his stuff for school, gave him shoes for basketball, and bailed his mom out of jail.

I do think Justin is as sorry as he says he is. That night ruined him too. You can see him struggling. But sorry is too little too late. What he did, he can't take back. He can't make right. He can't change. And he has to live with the consequences of that, one being that he really is left completely alone.

When Seth chokes Justin, he has nowhere left to go. After accusing Bryce of rape, Justin doesn't ask him for help, even when Bryce offers him a way out. After Justin tells Bryce about the tapes, Bryce says, "You know the real story, right? You know what's true." And Justin stands a little straighter and says, "I do now." When Bryce asks if he'll see him around, Justin answers, "No, I don't think you will."

Way to go, Justin. Letting Bryce buy you a bottle of vodka? Not such a good decision. Refusing to go crawling back to him? A great decision.

Breaking Up is Hard to Do:
But Sometimes it Shouldn't Be

It took Jessica awhile to come face-to-face with the truth of what kind of person Justin is, but she finally did. And she thought enough of herself to kick him to the curb. After he explains why he's stuck with Bryce all this time, she tells him, "Are you seriously trying to make excuses for what you did?" Even when he offers to kill Bryce for her, she doesn't hesitate a single second about not taking him back. When he asks what she wants, she just says, "I want you to understand what it's liked to be raped. I just hope you never will."

From the night of the rape moving forward, Justin and Jessica did not have a healthy relationship. If you're in an unhealthy relationship, no matter what the reason, don't stick around to see where it goes. I promise you it's not going to take you where you want to be. Relationships and friendships should bring out the best in us. Not the worst.

Here's sort of a bottom line to keep in mind . . .

You should never have to choose between relationship and safety.

You should never have to choose between safety and integrity.

You should never have to choose between integrity and relationship.

Back to You, Hannah

Hannah shows up at Jessica's party after she tells Clay she can't. "Part of me knew that I shouldn't go to Jessica's party that night." And here are those good intentions again that she often had that never quite came with the follow through. Somewhere in her gut, she knew that party wasn't a good idea. And it wasn't. But for different reasons than she thought. Like Jessica, she couldn't see the twists that night would bring or, like Justin, her part in them.

Still stuck on wanting to be wanted, she was convinced that night would be different. ". . . parties have a weird magic. They're like an alternate universe. They make you believe that anything is possible. Maybe you do fit in after all."

While Jessica was busy making excuses to Hannah for dating Justin, Hannah had already made her own about coming to the party. She says a few things that are interesting.

- "I thought maybe starting over didn't mean cutting myself off completely." She's right. Isolation isn't the answer. But it's okay to be picky about who you choose to let in. Who you choose to trust. Who you are vulnerable with.
- "Maybe I'd been hanging with the wrong people." Yes, exactly! But those are the same people she was going to find at the party.
- "Maybe I could start over with the right person." Ah. Clay. Yes, Clay was definitely more of the right person than any other guy she invited into her world.
- "But another part of me couldn't help but wonder what or who I might be missing out on." She'd be missing out on a lot. None of it good.

In hindsight, even Hannah says, "But if I'd have known what was going to happen, I never would've walked through that door." That night in Jessica's bedroom, Hannah is stuck in a very bad position. She wants to help but feels helpless. "I had to do something. I had to make him stop. But I couldn't get my feet to move." After Bryce leaves, she throws up—less from alcohol and more from witnessing Jessica's trauma, which traumatizes her— covers Jessica up, and whispers, "I'm sorry."

Because Hannah didn't stop the rape, she blames herself. "That girl had two chances that night. But we both let her down. How do I live with that? How do you, Justin? How does she live with what happened?"

Time out for just a sec. Jessica had more than two chances that night. She had herself. Remember the difference between responsibility and fault? I'm not saying Jessica is responsible for what happened any more than I'm saying it's her fault. We already know rape is not the victim's fault. But we can't put it all on Justin—or Hannah—to protect Jessica.

Ultimately, we're each responsible to take care of ourselves. We're our first line of defense. And yes, we already know that Jessica and Hannah would've chosen differently that night if only they'd known. Sometimes that means we don't drink too much so that we're able to make safe decisions or defend ourselves. We shouldn't have to. We should be able to trust the people around us to act decent and not violate us. But we can't always trust that. None of this was Jessica's fault. But she could've taken responsibility for herself in a way that protected her from a predator like Bryce.

Sometimes things happen to us that we have to deal with. We couldn't have made any other decisions or changed anything leading up to it. Other times, we have opportunities to avoid situations and people who have the potential to leave us hurting and scarred.

Just think what might be different if Hannah had stuck with her original plan to stay home. Not that what happened was her fault. She didn't set out to cause any of it. But she wouldn't have been tied to any of the tragedies that played out that night. She probably wouldn't have even known about some of these things that happened. And she wouldn't have been forced to choose whether to deal with that kind of pain or run away from it.

RAPE

There are three things I want you to take away from this time-out. One—*rape is not sex*. Two—*rape is not your fault*. Three—*rape doesn't have to define the rest of your life*.

Rape is Not Sex

Rape is *always, always, always* an act of violence in the worst form. There is no such thing as "nonviolent" rape. The very act of rape in and of itself is savage.

For the most part, we're going to be discussing rape from the view of assault by a man on a woman. But if you're a guy who's been assaulted, this is for you too. It happens. And it affects you just as deeply. I want you to know that I'm not discounting you in any way.

Before we go any further, let's talk about rape in different contexts so we're on the same page.

Date Rape is Rape

No matter what a guy does for you or says to you, you don't owe him anything. Certainly not free access to your body. Your body is yours. Don't ever forget that. No one can own you. You own yourself.

- If a guy takes you out on a date and forces himself on you, it's rape.
- If a guy takes you out on twenty dates before he forces himself on you, it's rape.
- If a guy buys you a car or takes you to Europe then forces himself on you, it's rape.
- If a guy says he'll take care of you and helps you when you have no one else and then forces himself on you, it's rape.
- If a guy leads you to believe he really likes you and forces himself on you, it's rape—and he's lying. He doesn't like you. People don't rape people they like. Ever.
- If a guy does any of the above repeatedly with different girls, he's a serial rapist.

The *only* difference between a guy who wines and dines you and a stranger who grabs you on the street is strategy. A date rapist poses as a friend or potential boyfriend to create opportunities to violate you. He lies to get what he wants—you alone with him.

Bryce is a mix of both. He takes the opportunity presented to him (guy on the street) when he finds Jessica passed out at her party. He plays the nice guy (potential date) to keep Hannah alone with him in the hot tub.

Rape Isn't Love

Someone who loves you won't rape you. It can't happen. "Rape" and "love" are mutually exclusive. They don't—and won't ever—go together. If it does happen, it was never love. No matter what he tells you or what you believed about his feelings for you.

There is no place for rape in a relationship. There is no room for love where rape happens. This is called abuse. These kinds of relationships are dangerous. If you're in this kind of relationship, you need to get out. Don't overthink it. Don't explain away someone's behavior. Don't make excuses. Just. Get. Out.

Sex Without Consent Is Rape

The absence of a "no" is not a "yes." Sex without consent is rape. If a girl is under the influence like Jessica and can't make an active choice, her lack of resistance is not consent. It's not even implied consent. A girl can only give the green light if she's coherent and her brain is functioning. It doesn't matter if you'd had consensual sex before. Anytime you're not "with it" enough to realize what's going on, it's rape.

And by the way, if a guy takes you out and spends all kinds of money on you, that doesn't obligate you to sex. It doesn't obligate you to anything. It's a date. You're just getting to know each other and that's enough.

Friendship and Rape

The words "friend" and "rape" are incompatible. Friends don't assault friends. Friends don't violate basic human decency. A friend will never rape a friend.

I once had a client come into my office. Quietly crying, Marie talked about how she couldn't have sex with her husband. As I came to know her more, I learned that he was a good guy who treated her well, and she loved him. But she didn't feel anything when he touched her.

Turns out that her first sexual encounter was with a guy she'd met in a group of mutual friends. She wasn't interested in him. But he was interested in her. One afternoon, she was changing clothes in a friend's bedroom at a pool party. He took advantage of finding her alone and raped her. What a horrible first time. That would mess sex up for anyone.

Because she was slightly intoxicated, completely freaked out by what was happening, and didn't know what to do, she did nothing. Remember when we talked about flight, fright, or freeze with Hannah? Well, that's what happened to Marie. Terrified, she froze. Afterward, she blamed herself for not resisting. And, afraid of how it would affect her friends, she didn't report it.

But listen. This is important. The waves you might cause with your friends are not what matters here. If someone in your friend group assaults you, get help. If your friends are upset with you for getting help, they're not really your friends. And you don't want them to be.

Let's interrupt here a moment for an important PSA (public service announcement). If something like this ever happens to you anywhere or with anyone—*call the police*. I know you may be feeling a lot of things—afraid, confused, panicked, embarrassed, ashamed, or even numb and in a state of disbelief. And I'm not trying to add to the pressure.

You don't have to call right away. You can wait until you're somewhere safe and away from the situation or until you're with someone you trust so you don't have to face this alone. You can even take a few days if you need some time. But please, please, please don't let someone get away with assaulting you.

It's not good for you to let something like that go. Look at what happened to Jessica. She just kept hurting herself over and over to try and escape the pain. It's not good for the other people that person will assault after you. Bryce moved right on to Hannah. And who knows how many other girls he'd raped in the past. No way Jessica was his first.

PSA over. Back to Marie. This guy, this rapist who violated her, wanted to continue to abuse her. That's what guys like this do. Playing on her fear and vulnerability, he posed it this way. *You might as well be my girlfriend. We've already had sex.* Um . . . no, they absolutely did not. Rape is not sex.

But feeling isolated, cornered, ashamed, and guilty, she agreed. Remember when we brought up borrowing the rapist's shame and guilt? That's what Marie did. And that way of thinking brings on so many problems. But it happens. People feel stuck by what's already happened, and they don't see a way out.

Maybe it's happened to someone you know. Or maybe it's happened to you. It doesn't matter how you got yourself into that situation—get out! It's not too late. Forget the past and make a deliberate decision to take back control. You decide what you do with your body. You decide your future.

It took Marie several months to find the courage to walk away from that guy. Since that time, she's never liked sex. Not even with a husband who loves her. At best, she feels dead inside. At worst, she's repulsed.

I wish she would've gotten out right away and found help. The longer you stay in an abusive relationship, the harder it is to leave and the more trauma you suffer. But the important thing is that she did eventually take back her life. And she decided she didn't want to live with that guy's shadow hanging over her for the rest of her life. That's why she came into my office. She needed help to move forward. And she found it. You can do the same.

The Victim is on the Right Side of the Law

The law is on your side. It does occasionally happen that a rapist goes to court and gets off without being convicted. This is the exception. Most of the time, justice gets served. Predators do get held accountable. But first, someone has to speak up.

In the US, 1 in 6 women and 1 in 33 men have experienced rape or attempted rape in their lifetime. Almost half were raped by an acquaintance. Only 4 out of 1,000 perpetrators are ever prosecuted. That blows my mind—*4 out of 1,000*! If you keep silent, the assailant will not be prosecuted until one of his other victims comes forward. If no one comes forward, he'll continue to hurt people. And to get away with it. We see that with Bryce.

You don't have to know the law to use it. All you need to know is that you have legal rights. If you're considering pressing charges or reporting someone, you can call a law office and ask questions before taking any action. That seems a lot less scary than you thought, doesn't it? You're not locked into anything simply by reaching out for information.

Some attorneys are willing to do a free, brief consultation on the phone. You can also call the non-emergency number for your local police department. The officer who answers will be happy to have a conversation with you, give you the information you need, and take a police report if you're ready to file one. And remember, that police report leaves a paper trail going forward. If someone else ever wants to press charges, it's there as evidence that they are not the only victim. If you decide later that you want to press charges, you'll have already taken an important step.

When Rape Hits Home

What if the person assaulting you is someone in your house or someone who spends a lot of time there? Your dad. Your brother. Your brother's friend. Your cousin. Your mom's boyfriend. Your neighbor. Your uncle. Or the close family friend you call uncle. Being assaulted by someone you live with happens. And then what should be your refuge becomes your hell. Home should never be your "least safe place" or somewhere you're terrified to be. If it is, I want to tell you two things. I'm so sorry that you're living like that. And please don't stay.

Relationships, especially with your family, should never be scary. Getting along with people should never come with the expectation that you to sacrifice yourself for someone else. Some families have a rule—spoken or unspoken—that says family sticks together at any cost. Family members usually have a shared loyalty. That's true. But when it only goes one way, where you have to be loyal to someone who's not loyal to you, that's not right. No matter what you're told or how you've been raised, it's not normal. And it's so not okay.

Let's look at it logically. Real relationships, healthy relationships, are all about people helping each other, being there for each other, and bringing out the best in each other. Being loyal to someone who's not loyal to you isn't that—because it's out of balance. It's also toxic and destructive. Don't be loyal to someone who isn't loyal to you or to someone who doesn't care about you. Do what you have to do to be safe.

Don't waste your energy trying to figure out or understand why a person assaulted you either. There is no good reason and no justification for violating someone. Even if you find out why, it won't change anything. There's nothing that person could say that would make you think, *Oh, I get it. Now I understand why you did this.* Nothing that would ever make it okay.

If you're living in a scary situation, tell the police or go to someone you trust. If you're over eighteen, find another place to live where you are safe and where you feel safe. Then consider either pressing charges or at least filing a police report to have it on record. And put the person who is hurting you out of your life. That's a big one. Don't look back.

If you're under eighteen, it's more complicated. Your options for leaving are limited. But that doesn't mean you have to stay and continue being hurt. If you trust your mom or dad or another adult, go to them. A lot of people don't reach out for help because they're afraid they won't be believed or that they'll be blamed for what's happening, putting them in a worse situation. That's a horrible thought and a scary place to be in. It's like screaming for help when you're drowning and having the lifeguard push your head under the water. Absolutely terrifying.

But here's the thing. Like we talked about before, you have a right to protect yourself. Sometimes you're the only one who can. As heartbreaking as it can be to ask for help and not be believed or, worse, be blamed, don't stop asking. Tell someone else and someone else and someone else—until you find someone willing to step into your corner. It might be your older brother or sister, a friend's mom or dad, a teacher, a coach, a neighbor, or someone at church or work. It might need to be the police. But don't quit fighting for yourself until you get help. It's hard, but you are so worth it. This is your body. Your life. Your future. You deserve to be safe.

Okay, you're thinking, but what if it's not your "real" family? What if you're in a foster home? If someone in your foster home is hurting you, tell someone. Too many foster kids put up with abuse because of fear . . . not only the fears we already talked about but the fear of having to move yet again. This is not a family where you are going to feel safe and connected. And you won't always be in this situation. One day you'll turn eighteen and have more choices. In the meantime, talk to a safe adult who can help you get out of the abusive environment. If the first adult doesn't take you seriously, talk to another. Don't stay without your voice.

Did you know that people who work with minors—teachers, counselors and therapists, social workers, healthcare providers, CASA workers, etc.—are "mandated reporters"? This means they're required by law to report it if a minor says they're being abused or hurt. These people don't decide whether what you've said is true or find out exactly what happened or why. They tell the authorities and let them take it from there. Sometimes the police step in. Sometimes they don't. But the incident is at least reported, leaving that paper trail we talked about in case that person is accused again. And in most cases where necessary, action is taken to get the minor safe.

Don't let yourself continue to be mistreated because you feel like you have no choice. There are choices. You may not see them but someone else might. My hope is that you'll stand up for yourself and get help and, in the process, turn in the perpetrator so they can be held accountable.

Sexual Harassment

What if what happens to you is not actual rape? It's still an assault and a violation. Words or actions that make you uncomfortable or that are sexually intrusive fall into the category of sexual harassment. When Marcus put his hand up Hannah's skirt at the diner? Sexual harassment. When Bryce grabbed Hannah's butt at the store? Sexual harassment.

Sexual harassment is:
- vulgar or suggestive comments, gestures, or facial expressions
- comments intended to intimidate, humiliate, or make you uncomfortable
- touching you sexually or in any way you have not invited
- continuing to go after you when you've expressed a lack of interest
- stalking

Sexual harassment is not:

- a request to get to know you
- an offer to take you out on a date
- a compliment (unless it's vulgar or sexually rude)
- chivalry (having the door held for you, an offer to carry something, or other acts of kindness)

If someone makes you uncomfortable by doing anything on the second list, you have the right to ask them to stop. Most people do those kinds of things to be nice because they like you. Someone liking you is not harassment. But if you tell them you don't like them and they refuse to get the *message*, that can turn into harassment.

Once when I was standing in line at a local deli, the man in front of me, probably in his 50s, was trying to pick up the high school student working the cash register. First—gross. Second—totally illegal. The guy was old enough to be her father. And more than old enough to know better.

He asked her to the movies. Uneasy and obviously uninterested, her cheeks flushed, and she shook her head, avoiding eye contact. Disregarding her "no," he kept on intrusively, practically begging her, making her more and more flustered and uncomfortable. His begging became harassment.

She could've called over her manager. A good employer would've intervened. But she didn't. I'm guessing she, like many young women, either don't know their rights or are afraid to say anything. She probably didn't want to get in trouble. However, that customer's inappropriate advances were not her fault. She didn't do anything wrong. No one should be put in that position. Don't be afraid to keep yourself safe. You have the right to protect yourself. Sexual harassment has specific laws and parameters.

I debated whether or not to say something to the man in her defense, but I didn't. Probably not the best choice on my part. She clearly felt unable to stand up for herself. I did call the store later that day, asked for the manager, and told him what had happened. I told him the girl had done nothing wrong, the man was entirely out of line, and that she had legal rights to be protected in the workplace. Hopefully, the store manager did the right thing and banned the man from the store.

Speaking of Your Job

If you're being harassed and made to feel uncomfortable or unsafe at work, you have options. As you get older and have a more 9-to-5 kind of job, you can go straight to human resources. There's a formal process for filing a sexual harassment claim and laws to protect you. I realize that might not help with the type of job you have in high school. In this case, start with your supervisor.

Can reporting someone make it worse? Sometimes, yes. But if the person you reported does something to get back at you, the law will protect you from their retaliation. This is called retaliation and reprisal. Yes, you'll have to report the retaliation too. And you can't do that until after it happens. Which is the bad part of all of this. But according to the law, that person can then be fired— because of his behavior *not* because you reported his behavior. In other words, people are accountable for the consequences of their own actions.

I've given you some "ideal world" examples. Sadly, we don't

always live in an ideal world or have a good work situation. You might report someone and be ignored. Or worse. Or maybe the perpetrator is your boss. Then it's up to you to protect yourself. Sometimes that can mean leaving your job and finding a different place to work. Once you're gone you can decide whether to take legal action or not. The important thing is to remove yourself from a bad situation. You have a right to feel safe wherever you are—work, school, home, and everywhere else.

On Being a Woman

Please don't take this next part as me coming across as sexist or genderist or any of those things. Put that aside for a moment. I just want to point out, that for the most part, girls are often raised differently than boys and given different expectations. I'm not saying it's right or wrong, I'm just saying that's how it is.

Generally, girls are taught to be kind, polite, caring, put other people's feelings first, and to play fair. Boys aren't. Let's look at that contrast in a horror movie scenario. Here's the setup. The killer breaks into a house and hides behind the door to ambush the person who lives there.

A girl walks in. The killer lunges at her. Her first reflex isn't offense. It's defense. She backs up and screams—or freezes—and plays by the rules she was taught. She doesn't want to hurt anybody. Without a counterattack, he overpowers her and . . . we've all seen what happens next. No more girl.

A guy walks in. The killer lunges at him. His first reflex is offense. He doesn't care if he has to hurt someone. He turns around swinging, counterattacks, and prepares to take down the killer. In his mind, there are no rules. He does what's needed to neutralize the threat.

It doesn't always happen this way. Girls can be strong. Guys can be weak. But it's the head space I'm really talking about. Boys are taught to fight back. Girls aren't. And your average high school girl probably won't. I'm a huge believer in self-defense classes. It can help us to be more prepared, more confident, and to learn to do what it takes to keep ourselves safe.

More on Throwing Out a Fair Fight

On March 5, 2017, thirty-six-year-old Kelly Herron went out for a long training run in a popular local park. Four miles in, she paused for a bathroom break. A homeless man, who she had no way of knowing was also a registered sex offender, was hiding in one of the stalls. He immediately took her down.

Having taken a self-defense class three weeks earlier, her first thought wasn't to go on the defense. Her first thought was *this doesn't have to be a fair fight*. She had a right to do anything and everything to protect herself. Things she'd learned in the class, such as "put hard bones in soft fleshy places" came to mind.

As she started losing consciousness, she shifted into an all-out fight, repeatedly screaming, "Not today motherf***er!" He punched her, and she whacked the side of his head with the side of her hand, clawed his face, and punched him back. Blood gushing from her face, she escaped and ran out of the bathroom. If you do a search for her story, you can see the red lines on the map from her Garmin that reflect how intense the forty-five-minute battle was.

A person walking by helped her lock him in the bathroom, and they called 911. He was arrested, prosecuted, and sentenced to prison. And Kelly went on to create Not Today (NTMF)—bet you can guess what it means—to inspire and empower other women to protect themselves. NTMF has a Facebook page as well, where you can see the Garmin map. Seriously, check it out. It's incredible. In July 2018, Kelly was notified her assailant died in prison. She and other women are breathing more easily knowing that he's forever gone.

Life After Rape

Rape can be disorienting and leave you reeling, stunned, terrified, helpless, and broken. And those aren't even all the adjectives to describe the aftermath. Rape impacts how you do life going forward. How you do everything, really. It shapes the way you see the world and everyone in it. But it doesn't have to.

Some girls feel helpless and stay helpless. It also sets them up to be taken advantage of again. Why? Because monsters look for victims. An abuser looks for someone who will be easy to abuse.

The way we carry ourselves reflects how we see ourselves. A girl who feels helpless and powerless inside will carry herself that way on the outside. Pay attention to the message you're sending. Even if you're terrified, stand up straight and act confident. If you notice someone watching you, look them in the eye, even if only briefly. It sends the message that you're not an easy target. And human predators, like animal predators, will go after the easy "kill" first.

Some girls vow that no one will ever hurt them again. They

become hard, invulnerable, and unwilling to let down their guard with anyone. A friend of mind in college used to say, "There's nothing harder than a hard woman." When we lose our ability to love and be loved and give and receive affection, we lose a part of our soul. Humans were made to connect. Being hard is not the same as being strong. A girl can be strong and soft at the same time. Just like a guy can be strong and kind at the same time.

Some girls have a sense of repulsion to being touched. Even by someone they love—like Marie. It can be difficult to be physically intimate. Being touched can be a trigger to the trauma. But that can be overcome.

Your Past Can Move You Forward

In the 1990s, rape crisis counseling centers discovered something interesting. When women were helped to look back at what happened to them and talk about what they might've been able to do differently to prevent their rape, they were less likely to develop PTSD and relive the trauma over and over.

I'm interrupting here to make sure you know that I have never and will never put the blame for rape on the victim. No matter how a person acts or what a person does or doesn't do, says or doesn't say, wears or doesn't wear, the rapist always bears 100% of the responsibility and blame for the assault. The end. No questions asked.

What I want you to hear is that you aren't powerless. There is a way to take back the power you lost when you were violated. By looking at the steps leading up to a rape and seeing options they could've taken that might've stopped it, gives some women hope that they can prevent a future assault. That gives them back control over their lives. And control helps us not feel so vulnerable. Does that make sense?

For some people, confronting their rapist—in a safe setting—can be a key part of healing. For others, this is either emotionally unthinkable or physically impossible. For many, taking legal action is empowering. But not everyone has the emotional resources to pursue legal justice. They just want to find a way to move forward.

Regardless, someone who's been victimized has the right to decide their own best course of action. The choice shouldn't be made for them. If you're in this situation and you're struggling with what to do, I want to tell you that what you decide today isn't written in stone. You can change your mind along the way. You can nix Plan A and move on to Plan B if you change your mind. But do something. Don't be okay with letting life happen to you. Like we said with Hannah, we can't change what's already been done. But we can find our power in what we do afterward. And it's worth considering all the options.

Wherever you are on this journey, you can heal. You may not have been in control of the assault, but you are in control of your life and who you want to be. It may not feel like it now, but you can go on to have a healthy and happy life. Women do it every day. I've seen how lives can change for good even in the wake of severe trauma. That includes finding intimate relationships and love. Give yourself grace for the healing process. Don't let someone else rob you of the beauty of who you are and who you're going to become.

Still have questions? Stay tuned. Coming up, we're going to

talk about how you can find help and healing.

CHAPTER 10
SHERI HOLLAND

"Some things just happen to you."
~ Hannah Baker

A single moment can change everything. "Sometimes things just happen to you. They just happen. You can't help it. But it's what you do next that counts. Not what happens but what you decide to about it." In this, Hannah is very insightful.

Sheri Holland is stylish, smart, fun, easy to hang out with, and generally does the right thing. She's nice to Hannah. She seems to be nice to everyone. But like Courtney and Marcus, when a bad choice goes wrong, protecting her image gets in the way of doing the right thing.

After Hannah sees Bryce rape Jessica, Sheri notices that Hannah is drunk and upset and offers her a ride home. Except when Sheri gets behind the wheel, she's a little drunk too. There it is. That one bad choice.

Drinking and Driving

Sheri wasn't drunk like Hannah, she was buzzed. And she

points out a little too much that she's fine to drive. But driving buzzed is *the same as* driving drunk. It's true. Don't believe me? Look at the science of your brain on alcohol.

It's fact that drinking slows the central nervous system and compromises your brain's abilities. One of the ways it does that is to mess with your response time. You may not notice or feel the difference. There's a lot we don't notice when we're buzzed or drunk. A lot we regret "the morning after." And when it comes to driving, it only takes a one-second delay to create a catastrophe. One single second.

Potentially, nothing could've happened when Sheri slid behind the wheel. You've seen it with your friends. And that's scary because it makes you think you're safe. But it's a false sense of security. It's so easy to think that *you're* the exception to "don't drink and drive." That the rules don't apply to *you*. That nothing will happen to *you*. Whether or not you feel bulletproof, you're not. Your dumb decisions will eventually catch up to you. You're not the exception to the laws of nature. You're also not the exception to the actual law or the very real consequences of your actions. No one is.

According to madd.org, every 2 minutes someone is injured in a drunk driving crash and every 51 minutes, someone is killed. Drunk/buzzed driving is still the #1 cause of death on the roadways. And, unfortunately, teens are a big contributor to that. Driving buzzed is playing roulette with the odds. And the odds are not ever in your favor. Taking risks doesn't just put you in danger, it puts everyone in your car and around your car in danger. You're not just gambling with your own life. You're gambling with other people's lives as well. And just what exactly gives you the right to do that?

For Sheri, the worst thing does actually happen. And it happens to a nice girl who, for the most part, makes extremely good decisions. She doesn't set out to kill anyone that night. She just wants to help Hannah.

There's No Substitute for a Clear Conscience

On the way home, Sheri offers to let Hannah "sleep it off" at her house. Hannah agrees but can't call her parents because her phone's dead. Already under the influence, Sheri looks down for just a second to reach for hers—so not smart even when you're sober—and runs into a stop sign and knocks it down. Thankfully, no one's hurt. Crisis averted. No big deal, right?

Wrong. Stop signs are strategically placed for safety. If there's a stop sign, it's needed. The one Sheri knocks down is located at a blind intersection where the risk of a collision was high.

The right thing to do is call the police so they know the sign needs to be fixed and that the intersection isn't safe. Even drunk, Hannah gets this. But Sheri refuses to call. She's afraid her dad will be mad. Afraid to lose her shining reputation. Afraid to be caught driving buzzed. So desperate to keep her perfect image, this nice, responsible girl leaves Hannah alone in the dark in the middle of the road without her phone. So many things are going wrong here, and it's about to get worse.

Determined to do the right thing, Hannah walks to the closest store—ironically, the liquor store where Bryce buys all his booze—and calls 911, only to be told someone else had already called. Back at the intersection, she discovers that the other person didn't call to report the sign. They called to report an accident. Not minutes after Hannah left for the store, Clay's friend Jeff barreled through the unmarked intersection, hit another car, and died in the collision.

Because Sheri got in the car buzzed, took her eyes off the road for a brief second, knocked down a stop sign, and drove away so she wouldn't get in trouble, Jeff was dead and the other driver, an older gentleman, was left seriously injured. A completely avoidable tragedy.

On top of that, everyone assumes Jeff was driving drunk and blames the accident on him. Along with his life, he lost his reputation, while Sheri kept on "shining." At least on the outside.

"I Made the Biggest Mistake of My Life."

The good news for Sheri is that eventually she owned her mistake. There was nothing she could do to bring Jeff back. But she finds the older gentleman who was injured in the accident and helps him and his wife while he's recovering. She calls the police and reports the stop sign incident as her fault. Unable to live with the guilt, she tries to make up for what she's done. In the best way she knows how, she "fixes" what she broke.

A clear conscience is a powerful thing. Nothing can replace it. If you have a clear conscience, no one can take it from you. There's a certain peace and self-respect—that you won't find anywhere else—that comes from doing the right thing. Plus, you won't be looking over your shoulder 24/7 hoping you don't get caught. If you've already done the wrong thing, you still can make it right. It takes courage. Be brave. Do the right thing. Get rid of the guilt. Claim your mistakes.

Negotiables and Non-Negotiables

Picking up the pieces after a tragedy is messy. No matter how hard you try to put something back together, it will never be quite the same as before it was broken. There is another option. What if Sheri had decided a long time ago that no matter what, she wouldn't get behind the wheel if she'd been drinking? Then none of what followed would've ever happened.

We make choices all the time, consciously and subconsciously. That's where you have the power to take control—if you take control *before* something happens. What does that mean? Have a plan before you're put into a risky situation. Pregame. Take time to think about what is "up for discussion" (negotiable) and what's not "up for discussion" (non-negotiable).

It's easier to work through options and situations before you're put on the spot. Chances are, if you wait, you'll almost always end up letting things happen that you never meant to let happen. People can easily be talked into things, or even talk themselves into things, in the moment. And once you get started down that path, it's hard to backpedal. One questionable choice often leads to another and another. Too many of those and you end up living with—or like Hannah, struggling to live with—heavy regret. Decide your non-negotiables now so they don't become negotiable by default later.

Sheri isn't clueless or careless. However, after knocking the sign down, she picks image over integrity. If integrity had been a non-negotiable with her, she would've called the police—even at the risk of disappointing her dad and getting caught drunk driving.

When Sheri comes face to face with a hard decision, she chooses "preserving her reputation" as her non-negotiable . . . and "doing the right thing" becomes her negotiable by default. If asked at any time up to that moment, Sheri probably would've said her integrity was more important than her image. But because she hadn't determined her non-negotiables, when it came down to it, she got it backward. Think through and determine your non-negotiables now. Committing to them ahead of time can be a lifesaver in unexpected moments.

Back to you, Hannah

Hannah calls about the stop sign but through no fault of her own, she's too late. She confronts Sheri about what happened to Jeff, and Sheri tells her they should stay away from each other and to, "Keep your mouth shut." She tries to tell Clay, but because of things he'd seen about her past behavior, he brushes her off. "Every drama has to be your drama, or it doesn't count. Somehow this is all about you." She calls to tell Jeff's parents what happened, but when she gets their answering machine, she can't get the words out.

Stuck and helpless and out of control, Hannah knows she's slowly drowning in guilt. "This was starting to be more than I could live with." But when opportunities come to get help to lift the weight off her chest, she lets them slip by. Hannah doesn't tell Mr. Porter when he asks how she's holding up. She doesn't go to her parents. She doesn't involve the police. And she hasn't set up her negotiables and her non-negotiables. Life just keeps happening to her.

The things piling on Hannah would make anyone feel overwhelmed. But instead of being proactive, she's reactive. And when she finally does take action, she walks the wrong way—not toward a place to get help dealing with her pain but a place of powerlessness where she can escape it. "By the way, I'm still dead." Yes, Hannah, you are. Because that place came with an all or nothing deal. Dead is forever.

FONDA L. HART

CHAPTER 11
CLAY JENSEN

"You aren't every other guy."

~ Hannah Baker

Clay is a good guy. And though Hannah doesn't always treat him that way, she knows it. "Clay, Helmet, your name doesn't belong on this list." She's drawn to qualities in him that she can't find in anyone else. I've always admired you. You are who you are, and you don't care."

Wrongly taking on all the responsibility for not being there for Hannah, Clay doesn't see himself that way. Later he tells Tony, "I'm just like everyone else." But whether Clay realizes it or not, she's right about him. He has a code—a clear sense of right and wrong—and he lives according to it most of the time.

A "do the right thing" kind of a guy, a bit of a nerd, Clay is genuinely true to himself. He doesn't try to be friends with people he doesn't like. And he's respected for that. Kat calls him a prize. Even Bryce calls him "squeaky clean."

Really, the only thing Clay does wrong when it comes to

Hannah is something that he doesn't do—step up and admit his feelings for her. Not because he doesn't want to. But girls get him all tangled up inside. Especially the girl he really likes.

The way he gets ready for Jessica's party, hoping Hannah will show, sums it up pretty well. As he tries on a shirt, accidentally puts on too much cologne, and checks himself out in the mirror, it's almost hard to watch him so nervous, so anti-Clay.

The fact that he's going to Jessica's is out of character for him. Other than the party at Hannah's house that Kat throws—where she invites Clay and bets Hannah he won't come—Clay doesn't do parties. "Last party I saw Clay at," Kat says, "Mm . . . my birthday, fourth grade."

Hannah's Third Story

Hannah has three stories to tell about Jessica's party. "I've told you about two of the worst decisions I've ever made, and the damage I left behind and the people who got hurt. There's one more story to tell. One more bad decision. And this one's all on me." Clay's story is the last. It's where their potential relationship sparks, peaks, and burns out.

Throughout the tapes, Jeff tries to help Clay win Hannah by giving him advice and pushing him to go to places she's going. Tonight, Hannah finally picks up on his involvement and teasingly calls Clay out. "You tutor him in academics, and he tutors you in—?" "Girls," Clay confesses. "Girl. Singular." It's the first time he owns the truth in front of her.

A little while later, after some seriously awkward flirting on Clays' part, he and Hannah end up alone in Jessica's bedroom.

There they finally share their first kiss, giving her a glimpse of how happy they could be together. "At that moment, everything was perfect."

Let's click pause here so I can point out something very important. There's a difference between Clay going to a party solely for a girl and Hannah going to a party solely for a boy. Clay's not looking for someone to "complete him" or save him or fix him. Hannah is.

During their kiss, she pictures everything right with her life—because he's in it the way she wants him to be. He's the source of her happiness. That's a dangerous place to put someone else. And a dangerous place to let someone put you in. Because no one can measure up. And no one should have to. True happiness isn't found in someone else. That's a hard thing to learn. Some people never do.

Projecting

Okay. Unpause. Fast forward to Clay and Hannah making out. She's finally with the guy she's liked all along. He's being respectful by asking, "Is this okay?" And it is okay. Until it isn't. "I wanted you to do everything you were doing. So, I don't know why my mind took me everywhere else. And I thought of every other guy. And they all became you." As that happens, she paints a picture of herself the way she thinks every one of those guys who hurt and betrayed her see her.

Because she believes bad things about herself, she tends to put those feelings on other people. That's called projecting. An easy way to explain it is this. Your boyfriend is secretly hooking up with someone but turns that back on you and accuses you of cheating. He's projecting his guilt onto you.

Hannah assumes the worst about herself and thinks others see her that way too. She does that a lot with Clay. "You say you love me, but you're always willing to believe the worst of me." But he never gives any indication that he sees her that way.

"I bet you wish you'd never gone to Jessica's," she tells him on his tape. "I bet you wish you hadn't invited me." But Clay doesn't wish that at all. He just wants her—the way she is. And he's willing to accept the good and bad about her.

But she can't see that. "You're good and kind and decent. And I didn't deserve to be with someone like you. I never would. I would've ruined you. It wasn't you. It was me. And everything that's happened to me."

When she pushes him away that night, he has no clue what went wrong. But confused and hurt and scared that he did something wrong, he leaves. After hearing the tape, he wishes he would've stayed, put on his shirt, pushed her to tell him what was wrong, pressed the issue. But she could've done things differently too. She could've said what she was really thinking. "Please don't leave." She could've shared how she was feeling about herself. She knew Clay was someone she could trust. But neither of them followed through on any of those things. Neither took a risk. Their communication—and their shot at a relationship—fell apart. Hannah called what happened between her and Clay "the worst thing."

Let's Talk

Throughout the tapes, there are a ridiculous amount of "near misses" when it comes to Hannah and Clay becoming more than friends.

They say love makes the world go 'round. Personally, I think communication keeps the world, and us, firmly on its axis. Communication impacts everything we do. Everything. I wish Hannah had figured that out.

Below are the four basic ways people communicate. Only one of them is healthy. Can you guess which one? If you can get this down, you'll be smarter than I was at your age, and your relationships will be easier.

Aggressive communication disrespects others. It's when you demand instead of ask, scream at someone instead of speaking calmly, or insult people in place of dealing with the real issue. Like Hannah did with Jessica. Yes, a really loud "f*&% you" can feel great in the moment. You might be right in standing up for yourself. However, handling a conflict that way rarely resolves anything. And it often makes things worse.

Why? Because people tend to focus on *how* you're speaking before they focus on *what* you're saying. They hear tone and volume before words. They're likely to miss your message if it's full of demands and insults because they've already tuned you out. Being aggressive or rude toward someone else isn't a reflection of them. It's a reflection of you. And if someone is aggressive or rude toward you, it's not a reflection of you. It's a reflection of them.

Next time you're about to go off on someone, put your

aggressive mode on hold for a moment and ask yourself this. Is your "right" to yell more important to you than the person you're yelling at? And, is this a relationship you'd like to keep? Aggression damages a relationship. If your go-to is lashing out, you'll eventually lose that relationship. While it's true that we don't define someone else with our words or actions and we're not defined by theirs, it doesn't always feel that way.

You know what's also scary about aggression? The belief some people have that if you don't see things their way, you don't deserve an opinion. Or worse. You don't deserve your right to safety or your life. We're seeing a lot of that right now. And it's terrifying. No matter what we personally believe, we never have the right to take it out on someone else who doesn't share our opinions.

Passive communication doesn't get you anywhere because it doesn't let other people know what you need. People can't help you if they don't know what's going on with you. It includes staying silent. Like when you refuse to stand up for something that's important to you. Or when you want to say no but don't. And if you keep quiet because you don't believe you deserve to be heard . . . well, you already know what I'm going to say. Everyone deserves to be heard. If you're not being heard, speak up. If you continue to not be heard in a relationship, get out of that relationship. It's not healthy.

Passive-Aggressive communication seems passive but is actually aggressive. Think the dreaded silent treatment. Which is different than actually being silent. When there's obviously something bothering you—but you refuse to talk about it—that's passive. However, if you have no problem punishing someone with silence, that's aggressive.

Has that ever happened to you? Say your friend texts you while you're in the middle of something. You tell her you'll get back to her, and she gets mad. But she doesn't say she's mad. Instead, she waits for you to text back and then ignores you. You ask if she's okay. There's no reply. You call. No answer. A few dozen texts later, she finally says she's busy now. Oh, she's busy alright. Busy punishing you for not dropping everything and making time for her.

Passive-aggressive communication is messy. And dishonest. It builds a brick wall between two people that makes it impossible to work things out. How can you have a conversation when the other person denies being upset even though they clearly are?

Another way to be passive-aggressive is to say something other than what you mean. Years ago, a friend and I headed to the coast for the day. Neutral, I asked her whether she wanted to drive or wanted me to. Pointing her finger at me, she smiled and said, "I'll let you drive, because *you* like having control." Wow. Nice. Now I really wanted to spend the day with her.

It was hard not to react, but I took a deep breath and got honest with myself. Did I like having control? Maybe. Was I a controlling person? Sometimes. As I thought about what she said and the way she said it—because tone and body language can really punctuate a conversation—I realized it wasn't about me. Not wanting to risk looking selfish for not wanting to take her car, she turned her negative feelings about herself around and onto me, making me doubt myself. That day could've been so much less stressful if she'd simply said, "You drive," and left it at that.

Assertive communication is clean. It's asking for what you need or sticking up for yourself without being rude or disrespectful—even when you want to be. It's saying what you mean and meaning what you say, respectfully. No hidden agendas. No twisting words. No being a jerk. And if the other person does the same, everyone feels pretty good.

When you were little, did your parents ever tell you to "use your words" to express yourself instead of crying or pouting or throwing a tantrum? They may not have realized it, but they were teaching you to be assertive.

Hannah is mostly passive-aggressive while Clay is mostly assertive. It makes sense then that they have some pretty big communication issues. Here's the deal. People don't automatically know what's going on inside you. Clay couldn't read Hannah's mind. No one can read yours or mine. Personally, I'm glad. Plus, that means we hold the power to say what we need and to go after it.

Be Sure You Want to Know

Speaking of communication . . . have you ever heard the saying, "Do you want to hear what I have to say, or do you want me to say what you want to hear?" If we're being honest, we all sometimes pick the second option. It hurts to hear the truth. But if we decide to be brave and choose the first, who should we listen to, and why should we listen at all?

The "who" is easy. There's an ancient proverb that says, "Wounds from a friend are better than kisses from an enemy."

Choose the people you trust and respect to go to for feedback. While they might say things that don't feel so great, their motivation isn't to stab you in the back. They just care enough to say the hard things that need to be said.

What about the "why"? Words said in kindness help you see things from a fresh perspective so you can become a better you. Remember that growth mindset? Having an outside, more objective point of view can also help you make better decisions to keep yourself safe. Other people see things in us and in our relationships that we don't because they're not as emotionally attached as we are.

Be prepared for honesty. And if you really don't want to know, or aren't going to accept what you hear, don't waste time floating the question.

Hannah has a hard time with that—hearing truth—even from Clay, who obviously cares about her. While she sometimes makes good choices to go to him for feedback, she never seems really ready to listen.

When he tells her that she should've waited to kiss Justin, Clay might've been a little jealous, yes, but he wasn't wrong. Stung by his comment, she tries Mrs. Bradley's suggestion to address conflict and says, "Pardon me, but you really hurt my feelings." The *words* are assertive, but Hannah is actually being passive-aggressive. She doesn't give Clay a chance to respond and punishes him by leaving without resolving anything.

I wonder how the rest of her story would've gone if in that moment she hadn't walked away and instead been willing to look at what he said in a different way—or been grateful that he cared enough to be honest. Unfortunately, honesty didn't seem to be high on Hannah's priority list. She wanted Clay to tell her something that would make her feel better.

Another day, during a lunch break at work, she asks him something she admits is "a super-needy-girl question." He's about to choke on his skittles before she gets out, "Do you think I can ever be as pretty as Jessica Davis?" He hesitates. Not because he doesn't want to shout, *Yes! You're gorgeous. I like you! I want to date you!* But because he's just a boy taken off guard by a beautiful girl who ties him up in knots and keeps him continually flustered.

When he finally does speak, he says, "Jessica's pretty and all, but you're special." He means you're more than pretty. We see that. She doesn't. She takes it as not pretty enough, getting up and telling him, "I saw you try to be kind and, you know, fail." Clay's left puzzled, asking, "How did this conversation go so wrong so fast?"

I think it would be exhausting and frustrating to have a friend like Hannah. You try to be supportive and your efforts are treated like they're worth nothing. It is interesting that while she says to Clay in the beginning, "I keep thinking you're a different kind of male, but I guess there's no such thing," she later admits, "You aren't every other guy."

And he isn't. He never runs with the rumors and doesn't base the way he treats her on what other people say about her. He bases it on his own experiences. Clay is what we call an independent thinker.

Leaders, Followers, and Independent Thinkers

Leaders by definition lead. That seems a no-brainer. But if everyone is a leader, there are no followers. And if no one is following, even the best leader can't lead. Having a certain personality doesn't make you a leader. Neither does being cool or athletic or smart or hot. And not everyone who leads should.

Look at Bryce. He's clearly leading people—right off the edge of a metaphorical cliff. Hungry for power and control, he abuses his status and his money to get what he wants. If people see you as a leader, take that responsibility seriously. Make good choices for those who follow you. And ask yourself if what you're doing is for other people's benefit or your own. A strong leader is *selfless* not *selfish*.

Followers by definition are people who follow others. Like Hannah, Monty, Zach, Justin, and Alex, at first. Is it bad to be a follower? Nope. But consider why you're following—Hannah does it to be liked—and who you're following. You can be a part of some truly great things under someone who's worthy to be followed. Or you can ruin your life under someone like Bryce.

Be picky. Know what you're getting into. Look for someone who believes in the same things you do and makes the choices you would. Someone you trust. Someone you respect. And know when its' time to have the courage to say no and walk away.

Independent Thinkers tend to process life "outside the box." They can be team players, but they're okay being on their own. They respect authority. And they have a certain degree of comfortableness with themselves and with what they believe, that gives them courage to sidestep the status quo. While they don't subscribe to the "the herd" mentality, most people still like them.

Clay is the only person on the tapes who doesn't call Hannah a liar, who wants to tell the truth from the beginning, and who accepts responsibility for her death. Trying to fix what Sheri did, he goes to Jeffs' parents and tells them their son wasn't driving drunk and that the stop sign had been knocked down at the intersection.

He also realizes he needs boundaries on what he can and can't handle. When Zach offers the letter Hannah said he crumpled, Clay refuses to read it, saying, "I don't think I ever could." And although it takes a long time, he's honest about how he's doing. When Skye asks, "Are you okay?" and he finally admits, "No. Is that alright?"

Yes, it takes Clay a while to talk about the tapes. No, he isn't exactly upfront with any of the adults who ask if he's okay. But he does plan on clueing in his mom eventually. "I promise I'll tell you everything but not yet."

I believe he's waiting for two reasons. One, he wants to deal with things himself. Back in 7th grade when some guys shoved his head in the toilet, Tony wanted to step in and do something about it, and Clay told him no. "Sometimes a guys' got to get through things on his own." And he definitely follows that—all the way to Bryce—when it comes to the tapes.

Knowing the tapes will never get to Mr. Porter if they go through Bryce first, Clay skips Hannah's twelfth reason and takes them to number thirteen himself. Then determined to get Bryce to confess to raping Hannah, Clay is willing to go to any lengths to make that happen—even taking a beating. It's worth it to him to avenge Hannah.

I believe the second reason he's waiting to share the tapes is that he's processing everything that's happening. In order to form a plan of action, he has to have all the information. He has to get the full story. Only he has trouble finishing the tapes. Tony tells him the others finished in a day and asks him why it's taking so long. Clay says that listening to them is hard. Everyone else goes straight into denial. But not Clay.

Tony, too, has the traits of an independent thinker. He has good relationships with people who like him and refuses to waste energy on those who don't. He admits his mistakes. And he tries to do the right thing—first by honoring Hannah's wishes about the tapes and then by realizing her parents need the truth and taking the tapes to them. "I tried to honor her secrets, but I don't think I did the right thing."

Hannah trusts Tony. She gives him the tapes and the responsibility of making sure they're heard. Apparently, she's comfortable in confiding in him, and that makes me wonder why she didn't share her pain with him before she took her life. Knowing Tony, I think he could've helped. I know he would've tried.

It's interesting that in all Hannah's talk of others betraying her trust, she betrays Tony's by using his recorder without telling him why. And he may never be able to forgive himself for not answering the door the day she dropped off the tapes. That's why he's so committed to following her instructions to the letter. She leaves him—and Clay—with a lot of guilt over something that's completely out of their control. It would be horrible to be put in that kind of position, don't you think?

Last up, when it comes to independent thinkers, is Skye. She keeps to herself and avoids drama. For the most part, she doesn't gossip, she respects other people's private business, and guards herself from being hurt. Seeing the scars on her wrists makes me think her journey to separate herself from the herd was long and hard. But she got there. And that's what counts. Having the ability and the courage to think independently will help you in high school and out in the world.

Situation Ethics

On the subject of making good choices, have you ever heard of something called situation ethics? If you haven't, all it means is that when it comes to your moral compass, you change how you act depending on the situation you're in. Instead of sticking by your "True North," where right and wrong are clearly defined, you decide the expedient thing to do in each situation.

While Clay is a stand-up guy most of the time before Hannah's death, there are moments after where he fails to stay true to himself. Here are some of the ways we see this. He steals Tony's cassette player, is rude to his parents, shuts out those who are concerned about him, sends the nude photo of Tyler, and gives in to being pressured to get drunk outside the store. He doesn't stand up for himself when the guys plant weed in his bag to get him in trouble, and he lets Bryce beat him up.

Fueled by his love for Hannah and a deep need to get justice for her, he sometimes ignores the potential consequences of his actions and breaks his own guidelines and boundaries. That may seem noble, but it can be a huge problem. Clay was lucky that his reputation preceded him. It saved him from getting into a lot of trouble.

A few years ago, my best friend from grade school found me on Facebook. She often posted things about "your truth" and "my truth" and the need to accept each other's "truth."

One day she posted, "Fight for the truth." Um . . . do you see the issue here? If truth is defined by what I want it to be—if you have your truth and I have my truth—which truth are we fighting for exactly? And if we're all fighting for our own truths on a global scale, how will we ever have world peace?

What you decide is right and what I decide is right may be oceans apart. Without a moral compass based on absolute and unchanging values, it's really easy to act in your own self-interest. That can become a slippery slope as one selfish choice makes the next easier and the next . . . until you've abandoned your principles altogether and given up your integrity. This brings us back to the importance of pregaming your negotiables and non-negotiables. And of a moral compass that points toward True North.

Truth is truth whether we believe it or not or accept it or not. We all have the right to our own opinions, and we can choose not to believe what we want. But that doesn't change what's true. And the cool thing about truth is that it will always withstand scrutiny.

Back to You, Hannah

Hannah will never know how much Clay loves her. She'll never have a chance to work things out with him. What might've been between them will never be.

Without the ability to "self-evaluate" and change how she related to other people, she had a hard time navigating relationships. Imagine if she'd been able to be honest about who she was—good and bad. Or if she'd been able to tell people what was going on with her in a way that let her be heard. Or learned to work things out instead of walking away. I'll bet her life would've been completely different. I know her death would've been.

CHAPTER 12
BRYCE WALKER

"An inspiration to his entire team, a friend to all, a tough 'mother-bleep,' and a true-born leader."

~ Hannah Baker

Inspiration. Friend. Leader. Principal Bolan reads those glowing compliments about Bryce during a pep rally where he wins the Captain's Award at Liberty High. Disgusting, isn't it? Those words should never be connected to Bryce. *Monster*, *predator*, or even *sociopath* is more like it. The guy not only seems to be missing a moral compass, he has no conscience, zero regrets, and he couldn't care less about anyone else. Not even his friends.

Do you know anyone like him? If you do, I want to interject a warning here—and please take it seriously. You can't change a person like Bryce by being his friend or girlfriend or by "being there for him." He's not a bad boy you can redeem. He's a monster. If you think *but it's different with us* and that you're somehow the exception to the rule, you will get hurt. I guarantee it. There are no exceptions for predators like Bryce. Please put your safety first.

Keep your distance from people who have no conscience.

Warning over. Back to Bryce. In addition to the other adjectives we picked to describe him, he's also what we call a "golden child." That person who can do no wrong and gets away with everything. Often a golden child is a bright beacon on the outside and a black hole on the inside. They're good at doing whatever they feel like and letting others cover up for them. Remember Bryce's #1 rule? "Keep me clean." Guys want his approval, girls want him—until they have a run-in with him—and even adults don't see him for what he is. So why do so many people buy the shiny lie?

Enter the Crony

To the adults, Bryce is Co-Captain of the football and baseball team. A star athlete. A leader. To the people who go to school with him, he's popular, hot, rich, throws all the best parties, and buys all the booze. He sets himself up as a leader. And followers buy the illusion and flock to him. I call those followers his cronies.

Crony is a weird word. It makes you think of the goon-like henchman in a bad movie or TV show—the guys running around doing their master's bidding with no thoughts of their own. That kind of describes Justin and Monty and some of the other guys when it comes to Bryce. Because he holds all the power, they do what he wants. In return, he offers them positions as his friends with all the benefits that come along with it—respect, street cred, drugs, alcohol, girls, and money. Or at least what money can buy.

People with no one and nowhere to go tend to Velcro themselves to people like Bryce. For them, it's a no-brainer. They need to be taken care of, and he takes care of them. When Bryce offers his pool house, he's meeting a legitimate need of Justin's. Once that need is met, Bryce doesn't hesitate to take advantage and cost Justin everything. He's forced to protect Bryce, compromise himself, and betray the people he cares about. All for food and a place to live. Jessica nails it when she says people like Bryce and his parents "buy you so they can use you."

Here's the problem if you're a crony. As soon as you refuse to do what someone like Bryce wants, you're left to fend for yourself. And if you're willing to bail, don't be so naïve as to think that person hasn't been keeping score of all your wrongs so you can't out them for theirs. Or worse, so they can blackmail you. The deeper you get in, the more risky saying no becomes. How far will you go to make a person like that happy? Are you willing to sacrifice your integrity? Ruin your reputation? Get into legal trouble? When you say no to your conscience and yes to someone like Bryce, you give them an enormous amount of power over you. Eventually you may find yourself at their mercy.

Here's something else to think about. Somewhere in this "friendship," you gave yourself away whether you meant to or not. The Bryces of the world only have the kind of power they do because people give it to them. That's a little scary, isn't it? Scary and freeing both. Because if everybody stopped giving them that power—if someone called the "emperor with no clothes on"—the power holder would lose their power. We begin to see this at the very end with Bryce, when people stop protecting him and Justin stands up to him.

Playing Defense

Bryce is shrewd and devious and has a defense for everything he does. He squeezes Hannah's butt in the store—after he calls her a lady to the clerk and pays for the candy she's buying. Go back to Jessica's comment about how Bryce buys you so he can use you.

Stunned, Hannah asks, "Did you just . . ?" And he comes back with, "Oh no, I didn't mean . . ." He laughs it off like it was an accident. At first. "It's just . . . it's real tight." And when she looks like she's going to get mad, he appeases her for a second. "It's tight in the store." Then he leans closer. "I don't usually listen to sophomore gossip, but for what it's worth, that list got it right." Slimy.

Some guys are insensitive. Other haven't been taught how to treat girls. A few are just stupid. If any one of them grabbed a girl's butt thinking they're being cute, they'd most likely back off and apologize the second she says it's not. But not Bryce. He enjoys degrading girls and damaging their dignity.

"It Was the Worst Day of My Life"

Hannah's "worst day" starts with her offering to take care of the bank deposit from her parents' store and ends with her stumbling home after Bryce assaults her in the hot tub.

Distracted by talking to Clay on the phone, she leaves the bank deposit on top of the car and drives off, losing money her family desperately needs. Knowing their financial struggles, she feels horrible about it. "It seemed like no matter what I did, I kept letting people down. I started thinking about how everyone's lives would be better without me." That quickly escalates into suicidal thoughts. "And what does that feel like? Like a deep blank, always endless nothing." According to Hannah, suicide looks like nothing, feels like nothing, and the signs are nothing. Which even she thinks is pretty scary.

To escape her house—and her guilt—she takes a walk. Nostalgia leads her to her old neighborhood, probably to when life felt easier. We all have those moments when we wish for things to be the way they used to be. But dwelling on the past only makes what you lost hurt more. When you long for something you can't have, it's like you're stabbing darts into your heart. Life can't get any better when you're continually wounding yourself.

Trust Your Instincts

Hannah's walk leads her to Bryce's house where she hears the "siren call" of a party. Even though her gut starts flashing danger signs, she doesn't listen. Ironically, when she should trust people who are safe and care about her, like Clay, she goes on the offensive. And when she shouldn't trust someone, like Bryce, she explains her choice away. "You think I'd know better than to follow that call after Jessica's party, but my feet followed it. My mind and my heart were still in the big, blank nothing."

Hannah knew Bryce was bad news. She saw him rape Jessica. Yet Hannah still went to his party. Sit with that for a minute. If you'd watched a guy assault someone, would you choose to go to his house *ever*? Personally, I'm out. Nothing would get me anywhere near him. Especially in a place where people are drinking. That's what got Jessica into trouble at her own party.

Hannah had so many boundary violations, but this was her most dangerous. It was like she'd forgotten all about her common sense.

Up until that moment, I truly believe she would've said her safety was important. So why didn't she stay far away? I think partly because she didn't have safety as a solid non-negotiable, and it became negotiable by default. And then she ignored her instincts.

Instincts are a natural sense of what's going on around you related to safety or survival. Animals live by it. It's how they survive the wild. For humans, instincts are more of a gut feeling warning you that something's not right. And then there's this whole prefrontal cortex thing—the part of our brain that's all about logic and thinking—that sometimes leads us to rationalize our "gut feelings" away.

Animals can't talk themselves into or out of things. They don't torment themselves with worry about trusting their instincts either. If a gazelle senses a lion, it assesses the danger and powers up to flee. Imagine if the gazelle said, "What if the lion doesn't want to eat me? If I run, I'll make a fool of myself, and the zebras will laugh." Or even worse, what if the gazelle said, "If I run from the lion, it might be offended." That sounds silly, but it's how we sometimes respond to real threats.

Has your body ever instinctually gone on high alert? Or maybe you just felt your gut saying, "This is a bad idea." Did you trust it? Ignore it? Was your instinct on target? It generally is. Your emotional—and sometimes actual—survival depends on it.

Knowing that, be willing to get out of a situation even if it's awkward. Even if the other person gets upset. You don't need a reason or an excuse to leave. Anyone who cares about you will want you to feel safe. I so wish Hannah would've taken this advice.

The Gazelle and the Lion

A lion is always going to act like a lion, and a gazelle is always going to act like a gazelle. You're never going to catch them napping together in the tall grass or trading places in the circle of life. It just can't happen. One is predator and the other is prey. End of story. It's like that with Bryce and Hannah—and any other girl he corners.

At the party, Hannah lets Jessica talk her into going into the hot tub in her underwear. Then everyone else disappears, and she's alone with Bryce. "I can't believe Hannah Baker finally came to one of my parties." He immediately compliments her, happy to oblige her need to be wanted.

Because that's what guys like Bryce do. They don't hide in the dark and grab you when you walk by. They give you a false sense of security and lure you in. They tell you what you want to hear. Worse, they *know* what you want to hear. They're scary good at reading people, assessing their weakness, and using it against them.

When Hannah goes to leave, Bryce stops her by telling her it's the best part of the night and that only the cool people are left, adding that she's "the coolest chick in the junior class. And the hottest."

Once he has her in a vulnerable emotional place and lays the groundwork for a false sense of security, he makes his move. Exactly like the predator he is. What's even more disturbing is that when she struggles, he pins her against the edge of the hot tub and talks her through it. "We're just having fun," he says. "We'll take it nice and easy." Watching him hurt Hannah—and then being so cavalier about it—makes me sick inside.

Fight, Flight, Freeze

"I know some of you listening might think there was more I could've done more or should've done," Hannah says about why she didn't scream put up a bigger fight. "But I'd lost control." In that moment, she says "it felt like I was already dead." When we find ourselves in danger, our brains and bodies respond one of three ways.

- we gear up to fight
- we get ready to flee
- we freeze

That last one is what happened to Hannah. Usually adrenaline kicks in and kicks us into survival mode—fight or flee. But in some cases, our brain and body get stuck.

We don't often hear about this third response. Some people feel panic but instead acting on it, they become paralyzed. When a guy moves in on a girl without her consent, she may not know what to do or may be too afraid to do anything. So, she freezes. He justifies his actions by claiming she didn't stop him so she obviously "wanted it." That's exactly what Bryce says to Clay about Hannah.

Too many guys take advantage of girls who trust them. Too many girls live with misplaced guilt and shame after freezing during a sexual assault.

Pure Evil Exists

Listen to how Bryce skews things when he's confronted by Clay about Hannah. Bryce starts by pretending to sympathize. "Sucks what happened to her." He throws out what Clay wants to hear. "She was a beautiful girl." Then he moves on to:

- "We had a thing off and on."
- "She wanted it."
- "She was practically begging me."
- "If that's rape, then every girl at this school wants to be raped."
- "You want to call it rape? Call if rape. Same difference."

Same difference. Wow. Bryce *is* truly evil. Excited by the hunt, he intentionally sets out to wound and devour his prey. And sadly, his "kill" ratio is far too high.

The Exposé

Why does Bryce get away with rape? That's easy. Because no one reports him. No one wants to go against him. And until someone does, he isn't going to stop. If you watch past Season 1, you'll see what I mean.

Near the end of the tapes, some of the people on them find the courage to speak up. Ryan nails what Bryce is even though the motivation behind it is selfish. "Why are we defending Bryce . . . I wrote a poem. He's a rapist." When Justin tells him to "stop using that word," Alex jumps in and supports Ryan. "Why? What other word would you use?" Justin does eventually ditch the status quo and face up to the truth when he finds Jessica hanging out with Bryce and she demands to know why Justin cares. "Because he f&%$*ing raped you," he tells her in front of Bryce and all the guys.

But it was too little too late. Things could've been so different if Justin had tried harder to stop Bryce from going into Jessica's room or been honest with her immediately. Or if Hannah had told her parents what happened to Jessica and never gone to that party. Because as we've seen, counting on Bryce to be a decent human being is out of the question.

Back to You, Hannah

Hannah and Jessica were both assaulted by Bryce. But here's where they differ. Jessica wants a better life. And though it takes her a long time to pull herself together and go after that better life, she does. She starts by breaking up with Justin, dumping out her alcohol stash, and telling her dad what happened to her. She takes back the power Bryce had over her and begins to move forward.

Hannah wants a better life too. But she lets what happened with Bryce act as the catalyst for the beginning of the end. It's the thing she can't come back from. The thing she won't let herself come back from. The night of the rape is the night Hannah starts her list of reasons and begins to plan her suicide. She gives Bryce power over her that he doesn't deserve. "There are two different kinds of death," she says. And goes on to explain that you're lucky if your body stops working. And if you're not lucky, you die a little over and over until you realize it's too late.

Except what happened to Hannah wasn't about luck. Before we talk about that though, let's just be clear. What Bryce did was beyond horrific. Hannah didn't choose to be raped. No sane person does. It wasn't her fault. On any level. And if you're ever in that situation, it's not your fault either.

I do think it's important though to point out that Hannah did have some power over her life, both before and after the assault. Before it happened, she made choices that led to her being alone in the hot tub with Bryce. She chose to ignore her instincts and the facts she already knew about him. Facts she'd seen with her own eyes. She went against her better judgment. After it happened, she made choices that led to her suicide. She gave up. And in doing that, she gave Bryce even more power over her—the power of life and death.

Rape is devastating and traumatic. There's no doubt that kind of trauma leaves scars. And we're going to talk all about that on the time-out on PTSD. But it's not worth dying over. I want you to know right now that Hannah didn't need to die to find peace. And neither do you.

There is help. There is life after rape. Your body and your mind and your spirit are salvageable. Hannah was salvageable. Believe it when I say that rape victims absolutely can go on to have happy, healthy, *good* lives.

Have you heard the saying that success is the best revenge? In a case like rape or other abuse, living and healing are the best ways to get back at someone who's hurt you. Don't give another minute of your life to someone like Bryce. Don't give them the win. Because by giving up, you let them damage you twice. You may feel like you have no control. But that's not true. Living is something you can control. If Hannah had waited it out, told her parents, given herself some time, and gotten some help, she might've seen that too. And she'd be alive to share her story of triumph.

PTSD - POST-TRAUMATIC STRESS DISORDER

If you have experienced and are still impacted by trauma, welcome to the part of the book on how to get real help. I've been mentioning this section throughout, and we're finally here. You have questions. I have answers.

What Exactly Is PTSD Anyway, and Do You Have It?

Some of us might think PTSD only happens to people in the military. The truth is that any traumatic event or series of events can cause it. Have you ever known someone who has PTSD? Have you had it yourself? Not sure? Let's talk more about it.

Because we've only briefly brought up PTSD before, we're going to take a second to recap and define it more deeply. In Jessica's chapter, we said it was a mental health disorder caused when a person experiences something terrifying or painful and feels like their safety or their life is threatened. Like Justin almost every time he's at home. And Jessica and Hannah after Bryce assaults them. PTSD can also occur when someone witnesses someone else's safety or life being threatened. Like Hannah when she watched Bryce rape Jessica.

But what does PTSD look like and feel like? Here are some things to watch for if you think that you or someone you know might be dealing with post-traumatic stress disorder.

The Event—something must've happened where:
- you experienced a single traumatic or violent event
- you witnessed a single traumatic or violent event
- you have repeatedly experienced traumatic experiences, abuse, or neglect
- you learned that something horrible happened to someone you know

The Symptoms—sometimes you:
- go into flight or fight (or freeze) when you're reminded of what happened
- feel like you're reliving the event
- have flashbacks or intrusive thoughts about what happened that you can't push away
- have nightmares about what happened
- feel numb inside—all the time or only in specific situations
- don't "feel" love for other people or the love they have for you
- feel like you're on the outside of your body looking in
- feel like you're "not all there"
- isolate and avoid people
- have a lot of noise in your head, and it's hard to feel "quiet" inside

- have a hard time being "present"
- have trouble focusing or thinking clearly
- have intense emotional distress over things that remind you of the traumatic event(s)
- have an intense physical response—weak legs, trouble breathing—to reminders of the trauma
- avoid distressing memories or reminders of what happened
- avoid people, places, and situations that remind you of the trauma
- are depressed and don't know why
- have difficulty feeling positive or hopeful
- are hypervigilant, looking over your shoulder to protect yourself
- never fully let down your guard, even "sleeping with one eye open"
- feel like you're going to die young and can't see your future
- see dark or violent images in your mind about death

Having one or two of these traits doesn't mean you have PTSD. But if you do have it, it might make you feel less freaked out to know you're not crazy and that other people feel this way too. These symptoms are just your brain reacting to trauma.

Trauma

All of us have experienced trauma on some level. It could be a "big T" trauma that was terrifying or heartbreaking or life-threatening. Like rape that left you with a fear of men. It could be a "little t" trauma that was not life-threatening, but still something that kicked you in the gut. Like being humiliated by a teacher. And it left you with a fear of speaking in groups.

Ready for some good news? Not everyone who goes through trauma develops PTSD. Everyone is different. One person can go through something horrific, regroup, and have a good, happy life. Another person can go through something fairly minor that completely levels them.

Some people refuse to let their trauma define them. They go beyond it. Others make their trauma—and their PTSD symptoms—part of their identity. "I had _____ happen to me, and so this is who I am." That goes back to that growth mindset we discussed. If you want to heal and are willing to do something about what you want, this section will give you some valuable information to move forward.

However severe your trauma was, you are more than what happened to you and more than your PTSD symptoms. There isn't a rule about how you should react or how long it should take to deal. Each person who experiences PTSD needs to work through it in the way that's best for them. What heals someone else may not heal you. And vice versa.

Your Brain on Trauma

Earlier we talked about how people who have PTSD sometimes feel like they're "crazy." Just so you know, "crazy" isn't an actual diagnosis. Whew. What a relief, right? Those "crazy" feelings actually come from the ways in which traumatic experiences impact the brain. Here's what I mean.

When you think a thought—good or bad—the neurons that fire alongside that thought automatically build bridges to neurons in your brain from previous, similar thoughts. So, if you grew up in a loving, connected family and life was good, you have superhighways of "happy" in your brain. That makes it pretty easy for you to feel happy.

But if you grew up in a negative family situation and life was bad, you probably have superhighways of "scared" or "sad" or "stressed" or even "angry" in your brain. That makes it pretty easy for you to feel anything but happy. In fact, your default or go-to becomes anxiety or stress or sadness. And unfortunately, finding the "happy" pathways in your brain can be like bushwhacking.

Just like your house has electrical circuits, so does your brain. And just like specific circuits are responsible for different functions in your house, specific circuits are responsible for different functions in your brain. When you experience trauma, something super sad or terrifying or painful, it changes how the electrical circuits in your brain work. In fact, some circuits can partially shut down as a result.

The chemicals in your brain and other organs can also get out of balance. You've probably heard of cortisol. In stressful and scary situations, the circuits in your brain tell your body to make more and more of it. Which works in the "flight or flight" moment but not long term. If you have too much cortisol, it becomes almost impossible for your brain—and you—to feel calm.

Research shows that children who experience severe trauma are more likely to have depression as adults. This is because trauma has changed their brains. Young kids who experience severe or prolonged distress often end up being diagnosed with ADHD. Some of them get in trouble for being oppositional and defiant and are also diagnosed with Oppositional-Defiant Disorder. Sometimes they end up on several medications to treat these various disorders. These aren't bad kids. They're kids trying to deal with the way trauma has "rewired" their brains. Instead of being given medication, they need to be given help to deal with the trauma.

If you've had serious trauma and sometimes don't feel quite "right," you can see why. The good news is that there are some things you can do to help change how your brain is firing.

- choose to think happy thoughts, peaceful thoughts, and thoughts of being connected
- spend time with people who care about you
- get out and be with people you like
- listen to music
- love on your pet
- eat chocolate
- watch a favorite or funny movie
- get active—go for a walk or a bike ride or a swim
- hang out in a beautiful, peaceful place and soak it in.
- picture being in a beautiful, peaceful or happy place, if you can't actually be there.

Basically, anything that makes you feel better helps you have more control over your brain. And if you create enough good moments, you'll pave more "happy" or "peaceful" pathways in your brain, which means you'll begin to feel that way too.

Being Triggered

Here's something that bothers me more than a little bit. Sometimes I hear people talk about being "triggered." But they're not referring to a trauma. They're referring to something someone said or did that they're not on board with. This is not the definition of being triggered.

So, what is? A real trigger is a sound or smell or situation that brings back what happened to you. The brain and body sometimes react as if the trauma is happening again, making you feel as if you're reliving it. And you'll know it when it happens. An important part of treatment for PTSD involves desensitizing the response to these triggers so your brain—and your body—no longer react as if you're back in it.

Back to the other kind of triggering. Being uncomfortable doesn't necessarily mean you're unsafe. I'm not talking about your gut instincts here. I'm talking about someone disagreeing with your core values and beliefs. Being able to hear and receive constructive criticism, listen to opinions we don't share, and come face to face with things that put us outside our comfort zone is a huge life skill. Huge. And crucial for surviving in our world.

Treatment Options

Just because you have PTSD doesn't mean you have to live with it for the rest of your life. It also doesn't mean that you'll never be you again. Every experience shapes us as we grow and get older. But you don't have to lose who you are. You can find a new normal. And good things can come out of bad situations—if you let them.

There are brain-based treatment methods that can change how your brainwaves fire, clear out trauma pathways, and get rid of—or significantly lessen—the symptoms. Sounds a little out there, right? But it's true. And guess what? Straight up counseling isn't usually one of them. So, if the very last thing you want to do is talk about what happened to you, you still have options.

I'm not saying talk therapy, or counseling, isn't helpful. It can be very helpful. But it doesn't actually change your brain, and that's the best way to get rid of trauma symptoms. Why? Because PTSD causes the survival parts of your brain to go on high alert. And rewiring your brain can calm them. Imagine no longer having PTSD symptoms. Imagine having your life back. It's possible! Here are some types of treatment that have a good track record when it comes to trauma.

EMDR

EMDR stands for Eye Movement Desensitization and Reprocessing. Don't worry, you don't need to remember that. And most therapists no longer use eye movements in the process anyway. Some use a light bar that you follow with your eyes.

I use a little device that has two small paddles—picture a cell phone in each of my hands—that vibrates back and forth while you focus on a distressing aspect of your trauma. This activates both hemispheres of your brain and clears out emotional or physical response to traumatic memories.. EMDR is phenomenally powerful in taking the "charge" out of the things that set off your PTSD symptoms.

Millions of people have been treated successfully using EMDR over the last twenty-five years. This type of therapy can be life changing. A simple but powerful method of desensitizing traumatic memories, it takes the charge out of a fear or belief that you've internalized and which keeps you recycling the trauma symptoms.

Here's how to find a therapist trained in EMDR. Do an online search in your area. Ask for recommendations from people you know. Go on the EMDRIA.com (EMDR International Association) website and key in your location. Alternately, you can check your insurance company for a list of therapists who do EMDR. Or even ask your doctor for a referral.

Neurofeedback

Neurofeedback is a powerful way of retraining brainwave activity to help get rid of symptoms and increase your sense of well-being. The name may sound intimidating, but the process is pretty straightforward. There are various neurofeedback systems currently being used. Not all of them can train the brainwaves involved in calming the trauma response. I use BrainPaint because 89% of people who've tried it have seen their PTSD symptoms significantly reduced.

People who have experienced trauma often have parts of the brain circuitry not firing the way they were intended. This causes some PTSD symptoms. Neurofeedback retrains your brainwaves to fire more in balance. It gets the brain back where it's supposed to be so you can start feeling more "right." Some people feel disconnected, like they're not fully there, after severe trauma, because of the way their neurocircuitry has been impacted. Neurofeedback, or brainwave training, appears to reactivate those circuits in the brain and allows a person to feel more connected to the people they love.

We're lucky to live during a time when we're learning so much about the brain and neuroscience. Not very many people have heard of neurofeedback—yet. But it's only a matter of time before it becomes a standard treatment. If you're curious about neurofeedback, check out the BrainPaint website at www.brainpaint.com. There's some fascinating information there.

Some experts on trauma endorse EMDR and neurofeedback as the best treatments for trauma because they can "rewire" your brain out of the trauma response and into more calm, more "normal."

Medication

Some people don't like to take medication. But it can be helpful. It won't "cure" PTSD, but it will lessen the symptoms and help you manage your triggers. You can ask your doctor about it or see a psychiatrist. Seeing a psychiatrist doesn't mean there's something wrong with you. A psychiatrist is simply a medical doctor who specializes in brain-based disorders that affect mental health.

And then there's self-medicating. A lot of people drink or take drugs to try and numb the pain, calm the fear, or cover up the memories or flashbacks of a trauma.

But here's the thing. Happy people don't drink too much or use drugs. If this is something you're doing, it doesn't mean you're a bad person. It does mean things aren't right inside of you. Self-medicating might help in the moment for a while. But in the long run, maybe even in the short run, you'll mess up your brain. And then you'll have another problem to deal with.

Have you ever heard of Amotivational Syndrome? Weed and other drugs can slow your brain to the point where you lose your motivation. You can't "get up and go" or get things done like you used to. Justin skipped school and baseball practice. He just didn't seem to be able to care enough to go. That's why weed is not a great long-term solution.

There are better options. Some of them are listed above. Some will be listed below. Instead of masking your pain, put the same amount of effort into figuring out what you need to do to get rid of it.

Mindfulness

Mindfulness is a type of meditation in which you focus on being aware of what you're sensing and feeling in the moment, without any judgment from yourself or your therapist. You just let it be what it is. It involves breathing methods, guided imagery, and other tools to help you tune in and relax your body and mind and reduce stress.

Negative thoughts tire your brain. So does denial. Both of those things also increase stress, anxiety, and depression. Practicing mindfulness can help you "center" and replenish internally. Some people believe it helps reduce PTSD symptoms.

Yoga

Some people believe that yoga is beneficial in relieving PTSD symptoms. There isn't strong research to support that, but it can decrease stress and anxiety. It can also activate the calming part of the nervous system and help you feel more peaceful. And it helps your body feel better too.

Other Methods

There are other creative methods for healing the body and soul. Some don't have any research behind them, but if they improve your life, it can't hurt to give them a try. Some examples are healing dance, art, aromatherapy, regular physical activity, walking, a support animal, and music. Here's an important thing to know about music. Uplifting, positive music can change your brain to fire in more happy ways. Dark music can't. While it may resonate with your pain and make you feel better while listening to it, it's absolutely not a positive influence on your brain or on your mood. Research has shown this.

When I was going through a hard time, my friend Allen told me, "Mozart is good for the soul. If you listen to Mozart for six months, it will cure your broken heart." Six months seemed like a long time. And curing my broken heart felt impossible. But I had nothing to lose, so I went for it.

I did notice that when I listened, my brain felt more awake and more "normal." And voila, within six months I was over the heartbreak. I don't know whether it was Mozart or time that did the healing, but I continued listening because it helped me concentrate. This is called the Mozart Effect, by the way. They've researched it and found that some classical music, particularly Mozart, helps regulate your brain and makes it light up more.

What's Holding You Back?

Sometimes people are afraid to get help because they don't want anyone to find out something bad happened to them and/or that they're seeing a counselor. You're not likely to run into anyone you know in a therapist's office. And even if you do, they're going to want their privacy too.

When it comes to getting help, your privacy is legally protected so don't let the fear of someone finding out stop you. Your doctor or counselor or neurofeedback provider legally can't tell anyone about you unless you—or your parent if you're under eighteen—have signed a release form authorizing them to communicate with a specific person or agency. Nor do they want to tell anyone. They want to protect your privacy and make getting help feel safe.

There's nothing shameful or embarrassing about needing to see a therapist or counselor. In the past, people were afraid to be seen as "crazy," and mental health issues came with a stigma. Thankfully, that's not true anymore. People are coming out and being honest about their issues. And that's a great thing.

We used to also believe we should be able to handle everything on our own. Well, if everything in your life was as it should be, you probably *could* handle everything. But PTSD doesn't happen in a vacuum. It's the brain's way of reacting to terrifying things that happen—often at the hands of people who should be protecting you. It isn't something you "just handle." And you shouldn't have to live with it. You *don't* have to live with it. You can get help to make it better and you are worth it.

CHAPTER 13
MR. PORTER

"You can have the best intentions and still fall short."

~ Hannah Baker

Kevin Porter is the school counselor at Liberty High and the adult who big time let Hannah down. I can't help but wonder what might've been different if Mrs. Antilly hadn't left. If Hannah had been able to spend some time in her office instead of his. Hannah and Mrs. Antilly had history. The counselor clearly cared about her students. And she was a woman, when Hannah needed the sensitivity of a woman to understand what she'd been through. Even Mrs. Bradley would've been a better choice. But that's not on Hannah. That's on Mr. Porter. He was the adult. He should've known better. And done better.

One Last Try

After the rape, as Hannah makes the tapes, she somehow finds her power in them. It's like the horrific reality of what happened with Bryce finally breaks her. It seems like in a good way. "I felt something . . . shift. I had poured it all out. And for a minute, just a minute, I felt like maybe I could beat this." And she makes the right choice. "I decided to give life one more chance. But this time, I was asking for help."

This is what I wanted for her all along. To get help from someone she could trust. Only it doesn't end up working out the way it's supposed to. And that's tragic. We'll talk about what went wrong in a second. First, let's set up what happened in Mr. Porter's office that day. The day Hannah follows through with her decision to end her life.

The appointment starts out fine. Mr. Porter tells her he's glad she came to see him and asks her what's on her heart. When she says "everything," he tries to draw out what's she's feeling. And for the first time, she's honest. "Lost, I guess. Sort of empty." Way to go, Hannah, for telling the truth.

Trying to listen, he digs deeper, and that's when she puts up the first big red flag. One that should've put him on high alert. "I don't feel anything . . . I don't care anymore." When he asks about what, she says "about anything." In those moments she spends in his office, she's teetering on the edge. It feels like what she'll do after she leaves could go either way. "It's like it doesn't even matter what you say. Maybe it does. I don't know."

Continuing the conversation, he asks her how she wants things to be different. And she raises more red flags. "I need it to stop . . . I need everything to stop." She clarifies when he asks. "People. Life."

Here's where the conversations get rough, and she loses her trust in him. When she tries to tell him about the party, he's awkward and doesn't do anything to put her at ease. Understandably devastated and traumatized by Bryce, Hannah has difficulty describing what happened. Immediately projecting whatever happened on her, he doesn't give her a chance to say what she needs to say. Making assumptions, he starts to fill in the details, saying things like:

- "Did you have an encounter at the party?"
- "Maybe you made a decision to do something with a boy that now you regret."
- "Did he force himself on you?"
- "Did you tell him to stop?"
- "Did you tell him no?"
- "Maybe you consented, and you changed your mind."

Come on. Really? Any girl has a right to change her mind at any time. And the school counselor should be in full support of that. He should be listening not speaking. Hearing not assuming. He makes it a point to say he isn't going to judge her—but that's exactly what he does.

When he wants a name, she's almost ready to give it. Until he says he can't promise that the boy will go to jail or that she won't have to face him. That may be true. But he didn't have to say it like that. He could talk her through her options. Be compassionate and understanding. Reassure her that it wasn't her fault. He does none of those things. And Hannah stays quiet.

When Fear Keeps Us Quiet

Hannah's reaction makes sense. She's vulnerable, scared, traumatized, and alone. Plus, if she gives a name, she's going up against Bryce Walker in a "he says, she says" battle she doesn't believe she can win. And who knew what he might do to discredit her.

She might not be wrong. As the school's top athlete, he seems above the rules. Here's what some other people have to say about how the athletes are treated. It's in hindsight, at the hearings, but that doesn't keep it from being true.

- "The jocks, they walk the halls like they own the place," Kat says. "The teachers feed into it. Bolen feeds into it. It's how it is."
- When asked about what school is like, Tyler admits, "The climate at Liberty High is . . . bad."
- ". . . guys talk at our school," Jessica shares. "They do things to girls that no one ever talks about and no one ever does anything about."
- Jessica also knows what's up when she points out to Clay, "Did you see what happens when girls try to get help?"

Because Hannah isn't being made to feel safe in naming her rapist, the conversation between her and Mr. Porter goes quickly downhill. Without a name, without her being willing to press charges—if she even can press charge—he tells her there's only one option.

Not true. There are always options. Plural. And with that statement, he slams the door in her face. His final advice when he finds out the guy is a senior? "He'll be gone in a few months." And "You can move on." His attitude cements her choice. Because Hannah's idea of moving on is to kill herself.

"Even if a crime can't be prosecuted, it shouldn't stay a secret." Clay's mom is spot on with that advice. Even though what led to that answer refers to Jessica, it applies to Hannah's rape as well. And it's something Mr. Porter should know.

When Adults Don't Know How to Do Life

We've been talking about the high school scene. Kids trying to figure out how to do life. Maybe you're assuming that once kids become adults, they've figured out a few things. That should be true. But it sometimes isn't.

Whether old or young, some people live life proactively. Others don't. Those who do have an internal locus of control. They believe they happen to life and use the power they have to make changes. Others live life more defensively. They may have a more externalized locus of control, believing life happens to them, and they decide to just let the chips fall.

And then there are the people who don't bother putting much energy into anything. They tend to take the path of least resistance. The status quo is good enough for them—and it shows in their work ethic. I believe this describes Mr. Porter. He seems more of a "sit back and play it safe" kind of guy.

All Counselors Aren't Equal

Mr. Porter wasn't hired to play it safe. He was hired to be the person who intervenes in crisis situations. But just because every counselor is trained in how to help a rape victim or a suicidal person doesn't mean every counselor is qualified to do it.

Counselors are trained to assess how "at risk" a person is. This is part of their job. I don't know what Mr. Porter is about, but I know what he's not about—jumping into the deep end to save a drowning student.

Did it honestly never occur to him that suicide could really happen on his watch? He's not a bad guy, but he is clueless. He missed all of Hannah's red flags. Signs and signals he was trained to pick up on. On top of that, he didn't offer or even encourage her to talk to a female on the staff. He let her leave his office without connecting her with someone else. Without even contacting her parents to set up a safety net for her.

When Grownups Choose to Protect Themselves Over Doing the Right Thing

After Hannah's suicide, Mr. Porter tries to cover up his actions. When asked if he saw Hannah the day she died, he says no. He makes excuses. "We all do the best we can." He lives in denial. "We shouldn't blame ourselves." He encourages others to cover up what they know too, telling Mrs. Bradley about the note Clay said Hannah wrote that "Unless someone asks, it might be best not to be sharing this."

In the last episode, Clay goes to see Mr. Porter and asks him if he wants to know what happened to Hannah after she left his office. Mr. Porter says they'll never know why she did what she did. Clay gives him the tapes. "There is a way." Clay's the one who plays the grownup during their encounter. He's the one who says, "It has to get better."

I will say, Hannah's tapes did seem to change Mr. Porter. As he listens to them, you can see him letting his defenses down. He knows he screwed up. I don't think he'll ever get taken off guard that way again. I'm hoping he changes. But even if he does, it's too late for Hannah.

Back to You, Hannah

Mr. Porter failed. That's not even a question. But in a way, she expected him to fail. "Of course, if you're listening to this, I failed . . . or he failed, and my fate is sealed." That's fatalistic. And can be a self-fulfilling prophecy.

Listen up. The grown-ups in your life are supposed to be able to shoulder whatever situation you share. But not every grown-up can be counted on to do the right thing or have the skills to help you. If you go to one adult and they let you down, please don't give up. Go talk to a second grown-up. Don't let someone else's failure leave you without support.

I wish Hannah hadn't given up. I wish she'd found the courage to tell her mom. Mrs. Baker would've supported her daughter, gotten her help, found out what legal action to take, held Bryce accountable. All of this would have made it easier for Hannah to continue moving forward into her future.

SUICIDE IS FINAL

If you or someone you know is thinking about suicide, let me just post this here right so you don't have to scroll down to find it.

If You are Suicidal . . .
Connect with a counselor 24/7
at the National Suicide Prevention Lifeline.
Calling 1-800-273-8255
or get on the chat feature on their website
<u>suicidepreventionlifeline.org</u>

"Suicide Is Painless"

Back in the 60s and 70s—when we had three channels to

choose from—a popular movie called M*A*S*H spawned a TV series of the same name about a military medical and support hospital in Korea that ran for 11 seasons.

In the movie, one of the soldiers becomes suicidal. On the basis that suicide is absurd, his buddies throw him a "last supper" and sing a dumb song to cheer him up. The director, Robert Altman, had two criteria for that song. It had be titled "Suicide is Painless," and it needed to be "the stupidest song ever written."

The songwriter couldn't come up with anything. Stumped, Altman asked his fourteen-year-old son to write the lyrics. It took Michael fifteen minutes. If you're curious, go Google the lyrics.

When Michael was asked what he wanted in payment, he said a guitar. He received a standard songwriter's contract instead. Lucky him. "Suicide is Painless" became a huge hit and the theme song for the long-running TV show. Robert Altman made $75,000 for directing the film. And his kid has grossed more than $2,000,000 in royalties over the last forty-five years—on the first and last song he ever wrote.

Is suicide painless? No. That's why the song had to be "the stupidest song ever written." Killing yourself comes with pain—not just physical but also emotional—for you and those who love you. Suicide is lonely, scary, and so unnecessary. Using it as an escape from the bad guarantees that you can never move toward the good. It's a one and done. There are always other options. Don't make suicide Plan A. Don't even make it Plan Z.

Deadly Shame

On April 28, 2019, twenty students committed suicide in a

region of India after exam scores were announced and many received failing grades.

Nearly 1 million Indian students took the exams between February and March of 2019. About 350,000 got failing scores, causing widespread protests from parents, student groups, and even political parties. In other words, one-third of the one million students received failing scores. Yikes!

The week after the suicides, the Chief Minister ordered the recounting and re-verification of test scores for all the students who failed their exams and urged students to not commit suicide, adding that failing the tests didn't mean the end of their lives.

According to the parents, *what caused students to commit suicide* was an error on the part of the software firm. Recommendations have been made to prevent this error from ever happening again.

Wait a minute!

The *error* did not cause them to commit suicide. The error was distressing, but each of those 20 students made their own choice to snuff out their lives prematurely rather than to address their concerns and find a solution. These Indian students were operating from an external locus of control. They allowed a huge technical glitch to determine whether they should live or die. That's absurd. The other 330,000 students chose life.

Imagine if those twenty students had taken a proactive step. If they'd gone to the school authorities and expressed their concerns. Or waited a bit longer for information. They would've found out that they didn't fail, they actually passed. Many of them would have gone on to be successful in their life goals and personal dreams. Instead, their parents and families and communities were devastated by the tragic and permanent loss. These twenty families are forever changed as they live out the daily grief of their loved one's suicide.

You are not responsible for what happens to you. But you are responsible for what you do with it. For how, or whether, you move forward. There are *always* other options besides suicide. Life is always the better alternative.

Reasons to Take Your Life

Recap

Look hard. Nope harder. How many reasons do you see listed? None. Exactly. The empty space isn't a typo. It's supposed to be blank. There are zero reasons to take your life. But there are so many reasons not to.

You know what people—especially people in pain—sometimes forget? That today isn't forever. Today, right now, you're living in one moment in one season of your life. You'll never again be where you are right this second. You're already moving forward.

Check out "Older" by They Must Be Giants. It's a fun song about the fact that you're always getting older. You're older now than you were when you started reading this paragraph. And now you're older still . . .

See? Life is always on the move.

Tomorrow, you'll be a day further into your future. A day further away from your pain. And a day closer to getting out of your current situation. Hopefully, you're also a day smarter. When you're hurting and desperate, try to remember that there's so much ahead of you that you can't even see. Don't miss out on what's to come.

Wanting to be dead and wanting out of your present situation are not the same thing. If you feel stuck, like this situation *right now* won't ever end, remember that's literally an impossibility. Time won't let you stay stuck. It doesn't stop. It doesn't stand still. Things can't stay the same forever—which means you won't always be where you are now. A new season *is* coming.

On the Other Hand . . .

Once you die, everything stops.

 Forever.

There are no tomorrows.

   No future hopes.

      No chance of moving into a

        better situation.

    No time left to chase your dreams.

All that dies with you.

Before you do what you can't take back, think about this. If you can wait out your "in-the-moment situation" and push forward even a day at a time, life will look different next week. Next month. Next year. Next decade. You won't always see things the same way. You made it this far. Don't stop now.

Everyone needs help. Life is hard. If you don't have a lifeline—someone wiser than you to talk with about life, relationships, sex, and whatever you wrestle with—please find one. Maybe ask a coach, a teacher, one of your friend's parents, an older brother or sister, your friend's older brother or sister, someone at work or church, or a counselor. Don't be afraid to admit you can't do it alone. Don't be afraid to reach out. That one small decision could change your life.

Pandora's Box

According to Greek mythology, Pandora was given a box that contained all the world's evils. She was told never to open it because once those evils got out into the world, it would be impossible to stuff them back in. Curiosity got the better of her—as it always does—and she peeked, unleashing all the evils. Only "hope" remained in the box, giving humanity a small degree of comfort.

Some people go through a lot of pain in life. If that's part of your life story, do you work hard at not crying because you are convinced once you start you won't be able to stop? Are you afraid of losing control? That, like Pandora opening her box, you'll release such intense emotions that you'll never be able to get the lid back on?

That's a common belief with people who've suffered a lot of pain or abuse. It's also not true. Locking down all those intense emotions is beyond exhausting. Letting yourself to cry and feel your pain and anger is scary. But it brings relief. Literally. When you cry, your body reaches a point where it decides it's had enough for the time being. You'll cry again, sure. But it won't be unstoppable. You can only carry something that heavy around for a while before it consumes you. Therapy can help you heal. Why not at least give it a try?

It Takes Courage to Live

I've heard people say, "I don't have the courage to kill myself." Actually, that's normal. Not having the "courage" to kill yourself shows your strong survival instinct. We're wired to live. Think about how your heart starts pounding when you hear a strange noise in the dark. Your survival instinct is working to keep you safe. If you've thought about suicide but can't bring yourself to do it, that's your survival instinct doing what it was made to do. And that's a good thing! Sometimes it takes more courage to live than to die.

Self-Harm and Cutting

About 30% to 50% of teens in the U.S. have done some type of self-harm. Cutting and burning are the two most common. 70% of those who cut have made at least one suicide attempt. 55% have made multiple suicide attempts. As Skye said to Clay about cutting, "It's what you do so you don't kill yourself."

If you self-harm, what does it do for you? How does it make you feel? Better, right? You can thank dopamine for that. Did you know that dopamine is called the "pleasure neurotransmitter?" When you eat sugar, you get a small dopamine surge—a "sugar high." When you use cocaine, you get a massive dopamine surge. Same with cutting and burning. Pain triggers dopamine. That's one reason some people choose physical pain to deal with emotional pain.

But here's the tricky part. Pain, like sugar and cocaine, can be addictive. Why? Because you eventually crash from the "high."

When you repeatedly give yourself a dopamine rush, you create a feedback loop that looks like this.

Do the Thing (cutting, binge-eating, cocaine) —>
Get the Lift —>
Feel the "High" —>
Crash —>
Crave —>
Repeat.

You can crave pain the way you crave chocolate or a drug. And like any addict, you'll find reasons—excuses, really—to self-harm.

Besides addiction, the other downside to cutting or burning is the scars. Scars don't go away. And they draw attention you may not want. Even if you're sticking to "covered-up" places, at some point you'll be in a sexual relationship and won't want scars "where the sun don't shine." It's expensive and painful to cover scars with tattoos. And even then, it may not look so good because of scar tissue.

When it comes down to it, cutting is definitely better than suicide. But you can be more creative than scarring your body. What else gives you a lift? Makes you feel good? Think about that now before you're tempted to pick pain. Have respect for yourself. Take care of your body responsibly. Find other ways to deal with your emotions.

Remember when we talked about PTSD? I gave a list of things you could do to help get your brain firing better. The same list works when you're feeling down or hopeless to. Go check it out.

What If You're Not the One Struggling with Suicide?

Have you ever had a suicidal friend? If you have, then you know it's overwhelming when someone says, "I'm going to kill myself." What do you say? What do you do? Who do you tell or not tell? How do you know they're serious?

First, absolutely assume they are serious. Let me say that again. Take your friend seriously. Don't take risks with someone else's life. You can't know if that person means it or not. And it's not your job to figure that out. Show up and be there. Be supportive. Talk things out. Offer options. Point out the good things in life because we tend to focus on the bad.

Second, realize that might not be enough. Your friend probably needs more than a "one-person rescue team." Especially if this has been going on for a long time. It's okay to be honest with yourself and say, "This is bigger than me." The responsibility for someone else's life is way too heavy for one person to carry. And it's not good for either of you.

Third, don't let yourself get sucked into helping someone who may not really want to be helped or who can't respect your needs. What do I mean by that? Say one of your friends constantly calls or texts you in the middle of the night upset. I'm not talking about once or twice or every few months. I'm talking all the time—to the point you wake up exhausted every morning. After a while, your grades slip, you miss work or practice, you get sick, and you're constantly stressed. Now you're having issues too. You feel like you're carrying the weight of this person's issues and the responsibility for their life and death on your shoulders. It's more than you can do. To function, we all need to sleep. Everything looks worse when we don't.

To truly take care of someone else, you first have to take care of yourself. You're the "steward" of your grades, your job, your relationships, and your physical and emotional health. That's where boundaries come in.

In this example, there's a lot of time during the day to talk things out. But if your friend only reaches out in the middle of the night and doesn't care what that's doing to you, it may be a cry for attention not for help. Like Hannah, some people get stuck a "fml forever" mindset and want company in their misery.

I'm not going to lie. It can be really hard to say no. But don't sacrifice your well-being to meet your friend's emotional needs. If you only make yourself available while you're awake—a reasonable boundary—your friend has to find another option. Like calling during normal waking hours. If they call at night, twenty-four-hour suicide hotlines are there for a reason. And the people on the other end of the line are trained to talk to suicidal people. Look for the number at the end of this chapter.

Any time you feel like you're in over your head, zoom out of your "circle of two" and get help—whether it's a counselor, suicide hotline, family member, teacher, coach . . . or even the police. When you reach out, you share the responsibility and the risk. When it's not all on you, it's less overwhelming, and more options mean more help.

Fourth, if your friend actively threatens to kill himself, don't try to rescue him. You can't. Call 911. The police are trained to do what's called a welfare check. Don't worry that he'll be "locked up" for mentioning suicide. That's not the way it works.

Have you heard of a 5150? When a person is suicidal and not able to commit to not harming themselves, it's a legal document authorizing that the person be hospitalized for up to 72 hours to stabilize. A 5150 is a serious process, written by a healthcare provider or a police officer, and only used in serious situations. Your friend would have to be unable or unwilling to keep himself safe for it to be initiated. The 5150 is all about protection for the person who is struggling. If someone is hospitalized and then starts doing better, the doctor may release them sooner than 72 hours.

Living with the Pain of Someone Else's Choice

There's a book called *After the Suicide* written for people who have lost someone to suicide. If you have known someone who suicided and you've found it hard to move past it, you may find the book helpful.

Here's a quote from the book that gives perspective on the person who tries to end their life. "It all comes down to the fact that if the person wanted to be saved, he or she would have told you, would have given a clear hint. But what suicides do instead is give out pieces of a puzzle. It is only after the death, when everybody's talking about it, that the friends and the family realize that they each got a piece of the puzzle."

What do you think of this? If you've known someone who suicided, does it ring true? If the person had wanted to be saved, he could've gotten help. But if he gave out little, incomplete clues to various people, who only put the pieces together after it was too late, there's no way that any one person could have had all the pieces and known to stop him.

If You Don't Do What I Want, I'll Kill Myself

So . . . what about the friend who threatens suicide if you don't X, Y, or Z or the boyfriend or girlfriend who talks about killing himself or herself if you mention breaking up?

There's a name for that. It's called manipulation. Manipulation is selfish. Every time you give in to demands like that, you give over the power to manipulate you again and again. When one person tries to control another, it's called tyranny. You don't want to be at the mercy of a tyrant. Control and relationship don't go together. Someone who tries to control you doesn't care about you. Holding suicide over someone's head is cruel thing to do.

I know a girl who dated a manipulator when she was seventeen. Liza seemed to live to rescue the needy. She liked angsty, moody "bad boys." Well, Allen turned out to be less of a "bad boy" and more of a "psycho" who treated Liza terribly. But whenever she talked about breaking up, he threatened to kill himself.

The last time Liza told him it was over he punched the thick glass window in her parents 'front door and almost bled out. She grabbed towels and tried to wrap his arm, while her twelve-year-old brother called 911. Allen survived. The relationship didn't. That punch was her final cue to get out and never look back. And it was a huge relief.

If you try to end a relationship and the other person threatens self-harm, that's not a reason to stay. In fact, it's confirmation that you need to leave. Want the threats to stop? Call the police for a welfare check each time that person threatens. Your "friend" will learn pretty fast that you can't be manipulated. It may seem extreme, but remember, your mental and physical health and safety have to come first. Make that a non-negotiable.

If You are Suicidal . . .
Connect with a counselor 24/7
at the National Suicide Prevention Lifeline.
Calling 1-800-273-8255
or get on the chat feature on their website
suicidepreventionlifeline.org

CHAPTER 14
THE I4TH REASON

"I started thinking about how everyone's lives would be better without me."
~ Hannah Baker

Are you surprised to see a 14th reason? Don't worry, you didn't accidentally miss an episode of Season 1. Hannah, however, did deliberately miss the next episode of her life. She didn't stick around to see what came next. And that is a huge, huge loss. For her future and for the people who cared about her.

The episode where Hannah kills herself is hard to watch. In fact, it was so disturbing that Netflix took the original scene out. If you missed it, be glad. I can't get those images out of my mind.

Femme Fatale?

For a second, right after Hannah finishes making the tapes and before she visits Mr. Porter, she has a breakthrough. A glimmer of hope. A thread to hang onto. But ultimately, she lets that thread slip through her fingers—and misses out on all the possibilities that could've been. She shuts the door on growing up, healing, moving forward, and leaving high school and her past behind.

While you're alive, there's always the potential for what could be. Life doesn't stay the same. It can't. It's fluid. You're fluid. Whether you realize this yet or not, things won't always be the way they are now. You can't stay stuck forever. But there is no potential in death. No possibilities. No chance to get unstuck. Because once you open the door to death, it closes the door to everything else.

Everything.

Else.

Now that we're at the end, let's look back and take advantage of the power of hindsight. What or who caused Hannah's death? What was her fatal flaw? In the beginning we asked what drives someone to take their own life. Is it one bad thing or 13? An impulsive moment? One choice we make? A path we walk?

The thing to remember is that just like you and I are the biggest variable in our lives, Hannah is the biggest variable in hers. And that's why Hannah is the fourteenth and *most important* reason.

One is the Loneliest Number

"Let me tell you about being lonely." Hannah talks a lot about being lonely. "Humans are a social species," she says. "We rely on connections to survive." And she's right. We're wired to be in relationships. Our brain circuits light up more when we're with people we care about, especially during meaningful connections.

Did you know that a hug, a deep conversation, or a chat that makes you happy is literally good for you? It helps regulate several parts of your brain and gets the "happy" neurotransmitters firing better.

Hannah didn't "relationship" well. She felt unconnected. "And let me tell you, there's all kinds of ways to feel lonely." Specifically, she talks about the kind of lonely where no one truly sees you. ". . . when you feel like you've got nothing left. Nothing and no one. Like you're drowning, and no one will throw you a line."

Hannah thinks she has nothing and no one. As if no one else listening to the tapes has ever felt lonely. As if she's the only one who does. But the thing is, she isn't alone. She just believes she is. She has her parents, a safe place to call home, and a few true friends.

Hannah's parents aren't perfect. No parents are. But it's obvious they care about her. In Season 1, it's hinted at that her dad gave up his thriving business to move to a new town and start all over again so she could have a fresh start. You can find out more about why in Season 2. But that sacrifice doesn't hit her radar.

Hannah's dad dotes on her. Her mom shares things with her and is actively interested in her life. Here are a few things her mom says:

- "Nothing you do is stupid."
- "I love you."
- "Have a good day."
- "You look radiant."

It may not seem like much when you read those lines, but do you know how many kids get told nothing? Or worse, get slammed with the opposite? Maybe you're one of them. Her mom's words are life-giving and intended to build up Hannah's self-esteem rather than tear it down. But she can't see it. "I'm not who they need me to be."

Hannah often thinks they don't see her, don't get her, and will never be able to understand what she's going through. Do you ever feel this way? Take a minute to really ask yourself if that's true. If you have parents who care, don't waste the opportunities that brings. As an outside observer, I believe with all my heart that if Hannah would've come to her mom with any of her struggles, her mom would've been there for her. No hesitations.

In fact, sometimes her parents seem to shield her from the consequences of her bad choices. And maybe that isn't so good. Maybe that makes it harder for her to take responsibility and learn from her mistakes. Consequences aren't fun. But without them, there's no incentive to do things differently.

There are many times Hannah tries and fails to make friends at Liberty High. Not all of those failed friendships are her fault. There are a lot of messed-up people there trying to figure out their own lives.

However, I do see a few reasons why her friendships don't work. She isn't very careful about who she trusts. She lets people in too quickly. She's missing some boundaries to keep her heart, and sometimes her body, safe. She doesn't know when to cut and run. And she has such a hard time seeing her own worth—and works so hard to make people like her—that it often has the opposite effect.

The other issue is that she doesn't trust the real friends she has. People who will tell her the truth that's hard to hear and then stick around to help her deal. When Mr. Porter brings up her friends, she says, "What friends?" But she had at least three—Kat, Tony, and Clay.

According to Kat, she and Hannah text often. Hannah could've called her. Talked things through. Kat appears to be the kind of friend who listens. And she knows Bryce. She knows all the guys in Hannah's life. She speaks the truth, repeatedly telling Hannah she has "bad taste in guys." Too bad Hannah blows that off.

Tony's over the high school mindset. He doesn't care what other people think. Even though Hannah can be drama, he genuinely cares about her. It's him she calls when her car won't start. Him she trusts to oversee the tapes after her death. If she would've been honest with him about why she wanted to borrow his cassette player, he's the kind of guy who would jump right in and start an intervention. We see that in his concern for Clay as he struggles to deal with what's on the tapes. Tony is on Hannah's side, even after she kills herself. When Clay questions if Hannah is really telling the truth on the tapes, Tony says, "She was telling *her* truth."

Clay loves Hannah enough to see past the gossip and to push past the obstacles she puts in his way. He doesn't always agree with her choices, but he never stops being her friend. Deep down, she knows that. She just never acts on it. "I thought I could never show my face at that school again. Everything was dark for days," she says as she looks at Clay. "Then just a little flash of light." She even mentions that "I wanted to tell Clay everything." But she couldn't get past the awkwardness of what happened between them at Jessica's party and chose to believe instead that "Clay

Jensen hates me." She carries so much self-loathing and perceived rejection. Even when it's not there.

The Big Picture

When I look at Hannah, I see a girl who's:

- a lot like most teenage girls
- often lonely
- sometimes sad
- longing to be accepted and liked and loved
- struggling to find herself and her place in the world
- dealing with the pressures of a "fishbowl" life that social media brings
- desperate for friends who care about her
- hoping life will get better

But at the same time, this girl who hopes for a better life also:

- sees life through a one-sided lens and expects others to "get" her feelings without trying to "get" theirs
- sets terrible (or no) boundaries
- often goes against her values or gut instincts and makes risky decisions
- has an external, not an internal, locus of control and sees herself as a victim who life happens to
- has a fixed mindset instead of a growth mindset, wants to hear what makes her feel good over the truth, and doesn't learn from her mistakes
- is passive-aggressive rather than clear and honest
- holds decent people at a distance and seeks out emotionally unavailable people
- has expectations that are sometimes impossible to meet

- tends to see herself as the reference point for reality, the "center of the universe"

What About You?

We've spent a lot of time with Hannah—in the series and in this book. Have you learned anything about yourself from seeing the world through her eyes? Do you see similarities? Differences? Are there places in your life you want to make changes?

Think about taking some time to really look at yourself—who you are now and who you want to be later. Sometimes it helps if you ask yourself some questions and then get real honest with the answers.

- Do you have a growth mindset or fixed mindset?
- Where do you feel stuck?
- Do you have an internal or external locus of control?
- What can you take charge of to make things happen and make life better?
- What are your negotiables and non-negotiables? Do you need to take an inventory and shift them around?
- What kind of communicator are you? Aggressive, passive, passive-aggressive, or assertive? What would help you be more assertive?
- Do you set good boundaries, or do you need to "boundary up" and draw better lines for yourself?
- What's already working in your life? And why? How can you apply that to the places you need help?
- Who's available to help you? Do you have a mentor or someone older you can trust?

Keep in mind that sometimes attitude can be everything. Our

attitude carries a lot of power. What you *feel* seems true, whether it's actually true or not. The same situation and the same obstacles can look completely different depending on if you showcase them in the positive versus the negative.

Fatalism

Hannah believes things about herself and her life that color the way she sees her world, affect how she feels about herself, and play into every decision she makes.

"There's so much wrong in the world. There's so much hurt. I couldn't take knowing I made it worse. And I couldn't take knowing it would never get any better." Hannah often gets stuck in some seriously fatal thinking.

Fatalism says there's no point trying to make it better because it won't get better. That basically we're powerless to change our circumstances. That things will always be the way they are now. That. Is. A. Big. Fat. Lie. Don't believe it. No matter how bad your life is, you're never completely powerless.

There are options. You just have to find them. And if you can't find them on your own, get help. If help is hard to find, keep trying. Don't stop after one person lets you down like Hannah did. Fight for the will to survive. Don't give up until you have what you need. Okay. Lecture over.

When Mr. Porter tells Hannah to move on, she assumes he means get over it. And since she can't, she moves on by leaving her life here behind. "I decided that no one would ever hurt me again." Mr. Porter screwed up, but in no way did he ever mean for her to do that.

Hannah tended to remember and hold grudges against slights, but then she carelessly allowed herself to be put in difficult situations by people who had already violated her trust. Remember when she walked to Bryce's house and joined the party, she already knew what Bryce was.

When the Will to Wound Outweighs the Will to Live

"I've made some very bad decisions in my life, as you know." Hannah says this, leading us to believe she accepts the responsibility, but then she turns around and blames other people. Don't think I'm downplaying anything that happens to her. Some of it is tragic and horrible, things no one should ever have to experience. That's not what I'm talking about. People wronged her. That's not in question. What is in question is how she spends her time and energy afterward. Remember, we can't control other people's actions. We can control what we do about them and how we react to them.

Hannah spends hours planning, scheming, and scripting the cassettes. "Get a snack. Settle in. Cause I'm about to tell you the story of my life." She takes time calculating and working on the strategic sequence of listeners—who gets the tapes first, second, and so on. She puts a lot of effort into mapping out the locations of the places each listener is to go—the park, Tyler's house, the fateful stop sign, etc. And in turn, she expects her listeners to do the same when it comes to following her instructions.

Can you imagine doing all this? Putting together and recording each of the tapes. Rerecording when you make a mistake. Making sure they coordinate. Remembering—correctly or incorrectly—all the details of each incident, interaction, and event. Dwelling on how people wounded you. Betrayed you. Offended you. That's enough to leave anyone drowning in self-pity.

How many hours did it take Hannah to put all that together? How much effort did she put into that project? Imagine if she'd put the same number of hours of energy, creative thinking, and strategic planning into moving her life forward.

I'm guessing she spent at least a hundred hours. A lot can be accomplished in a hundred hours. That's two college classes in a semester. A drive across the U.S. and back again. And if she'd put those hours into seeing a counselor or therapist, at one hour a week, two full years of therapy. More than enough time to find her way back to a better place, desensitize the trauma, develop stronger life skills, and empower her to move into the next phase of life thriving.

Instead, she spent those hours letting herself get lost in negative thinking. She created a legacy around her suicide. Had she invested all that time in a more positive and productive way, imagine the legacy she could have created instead. A legacy of life.

No Matter What You Think, Suicide Is Never Effective Revenge

Hannah premeditated both her suicide and the impact it would have on others. She set out to punish them for what they'd done. Ever have these kinds of thoughts?

- "I'll show them."

- "They'll be sorry when I'm gone"
- "They'll regret ever doing/saying that."

The thing is they might not. The people who hurt you aren't going to be as torn up and guilt-ridden as you think. It's harsh to say, but some of them won't even care. Think Bryce. Did he shed a single tear over Hannah? No. Her suicide didn't even register with him, let alone come with any kind of realization that he could be a potential cause.

Suicide hands the person or people who wronged you the win. They're alive. You're not. That means you automatically lose. Don't give anyone that kind of power over you. The best revenge is coming through strong on the other side. Showing them they can't break you. Think triumph and healing and victory.

Just what did Hannah accomplish by her death? I wonder what she could've accomplished in life. When it came to revenge, why did suicide have to factor in at all? Was there anything she did by dying that she couldn't have done by living? The answer is no.

On the other hand, there is so much she could've done by living that she'll never get to do by dying. A gifted writer and poet, had she had the courage to heal and to live, she could've been an amazing force for other girls to heal and redeem the terrible experiences they had in life.

Suicide is not a good form of getting revenge. But it is a good way to devastate those who love you. When someone you love suicides, there is no closure. There is unfinished business and it's nearly impossible to let go.

Back to You, Hannah

We've talked a lot about Hannah's path to suicide. But here's an important question. Once she stepped onto that path, did she have to stay on it, or was there a way off? That day in Mr. Porter's office when Hannah said "everything" was wrong, he asked, "How did you get here?" And she answered, "One thing on top of the other."

One reason on top of another—13 of them to be exact. And it sure seems that way as things begin to pile up. But while all 13 reasons, all 13 people Hannah calls out, have an impact in her life story, was any one of them enough of a reason for her to end her life? Were all of them combined a big enough reason?

In the tapes, Hannah talks about "why my life ended," saying to those 13 people, "you're one of the reasons why." Hold on here. "Why my life ended?" As if death just somehow happened to her, and she had no way to stop it? Sounds like an external locus of control to me.

So . . . is one person responsible for another's emotions? Decisions? Actions?

No. We're each responsible for our own feelings and our own behaviors. Going with that idea, is one person powerful enough to cause another person to kill themselves? That's a lot of power. And a lot of responsibility. And a lot of guilt to carry, maybe unnecessarily. The answer again is no.

Only the person who suicides is responsible for that choice. There is only one reason why Hannah's life ended prematurely— she made it happen. There is no "why my life ended." Hannah

Baker killed herself. And she didn't have to. Bottom-line—Hannah chose suicide. No one killed her. No one made her kill herself. Hannah alone decided to end her life.

When she made the decision ". . . that no would ever hurt me again," she ended everything that might've been. Maybe she and Clay would've built a life together. Maybe she would've had a little girl or boy and been a loving mother who understood exactly what they were going through. She may have written a book or several. Or moved to New York, or traveled the world, or stayed close to home. We'll never know. She's out of time. Because she made a choice.

I hope you've seen that dying didn't have to be Hannah's only choice. That life is more than one situation. That once you step onto a path, there's nothing keeping you from hopping right back off. That no one else has power over your life or your death—it's all on you.

There were so many exits Hannah ignored. It was like her feet got stuck going one direction. And that was Hannah's fatal flaw—her choice to give up and end her life instead of sticking around and working toward healing so that she could grow up and pursue the life she wanted.

If you're contemplating suicide, please know that you have other options. It doesn't have to be a done deal. Start by reaching out. Talk to someone. Get help. Don't give up. And please know that other people are not better off without you.

Anything you do, no matter how much it makes you feel stupid or humiliated or worthless, doesn't make the people who love you stop loving you. It doesn't define you. You are still you.

Even if you're doing or have done something you think is terrible and unforgivable, it isn't. You have the option to change course. To change who you are. Nothing about you is terrible enough to make the world a better place without you. Because you're still alive, you have a chance that Hannah does not—to make your future better than your past.

The End . . .

or is it your new beginning?

ABOUT THE AUTHOR

Fonda Hart has been providing therapy to children, adolescents, and adults since 1995, and received her MFT license in 2002. She has a passion for encouraging and helping her clients achieve a healthy outlook on life.

Having spent several years in full-time Christian ministry, Fonda also enjoys working with missionaries and pastors' families. She loves the outdoors and thrives when she's able to go cycling with friends. She also enjoys hiking and kayaking and would rather sit outside with a good book and a cold drink than just about anywhere else.

You can learn more about Fonda at www.FresnoCounseling.com and can contact her at fondahartlmft@gmail.com.

Made in the USA
Middletown, DE
14 May 2023

30565452R00126